God in Business—

A Common Man's Guide

$$R^7 = U^X$$

Helping you understand what it means
to partnership with the Holy Spirit in business.

Helping you bridge the gap
between faith and works—
between principles and practicality—
between knowledge and experience—
between what you do and what God does.

Ted Cottingham, MBA

GodinBusiness.com, Inc.
Box 33130
Tulsa, Oklahoma 74153

God in Business—A Common Man's Guide $R^7=U^X$

Copyright © 2001 Ted Cottingham, MBA

GodinBusiness.com, Inc.
Box 33130
Tulsa, Oklahoma 74153

The purpose of GodinBusiness.com is to help merge God and business and to build a platform for those who do.

Any experiences that you are willing to share with others via the GodinBusiness.com Website or in other GodinBusiness publications are invited.

Library of Congress Control Number: 00-091560

ISBN 0-9705709-3-7

Publisher's Cataloging-in-Publication

Cottingham, Ted.
God in business : a common man's guide : R7=Ux / Ted Cottingham. – 1st ed.
    p. cm.
"Helping you understand what it means to partnership with the Holy Spirit in business. Helping you bridge the gap between faith and works—between principles and practicality—between knowledge and experience—between what you do and what God does."

1. Business—Religious aspects—Christianity.
2. Management—Religious aspects—Christianity.
3. Business ethics. 4. Businesspeople—Religious life.
I. Title.

HF5388.C68 2000   261.8'5
                         QBI00-901585

Table of Contents

You don't have to see everything my way. It's okay to disagree with me; we can still be friends.

Chapter 1

The Liberation of the Common Man

We are beginning a new season: the liberation of the common man. All of our old rules are changing.

The liberation of the common man I speak of is founded on the growing revelation that there is no gap between the sacred and the secular for those who will partner with God to do what is in their heart. The walls separating business and ministry are coming down.

Many leaders in business, government and even religion, have viewed the common man as a means to their end and a way to get their own needs met. There has been little regard for the gifts and creative abilities of the commoners. We read occasionally of exceptions, but in the daily workforce of millions, the common man is kept at the lowest level.

But all of this is changing. The understanding of how our spiritual gifts are released to work in conjunction with our natural gifts, skills, abilities and talents will increase. Our ability to operate in the spirit of God will increase. Our love for others and the quest for the release of all of their potential will develop and mature, the impossible will become achievable, and God will smile.

We will see the rise of the Godly in dimensions and arenas yet unheard of. Miracles at the hand of the simple, common man whose God is the Lord will be commonplace. There will be increased freedom for the individual to operate in all realms in the power of the Spirit of God.

Godly leadership will arise. Godly leadership breeds leadership and raises the confidence, skills, abilities, and anointing of those around them. True leadership frees the decision-making abilities of those around them while still holding them accountable.

1

Everything we've put together as man and as church will be tested over the next few years. Everything that man has established is built on sand, and is on the verge of collapse. Everything that God has established is built on rock, and is on the verge of explosive growth.

There will be a profound understanding that we are part of something big—bigger than we are—that transcends all tangible realities and common understandings. And this understanding will motivate actions that others may think strange. But the outcome is yet to be seen.

There will be a profound understanding of letting God guide in our decision-making. We may do things that seem unwise and foolish. We may do things that look one way but are another.

There will be pure motives before the Master. The motive of hearts will be to please God, not maximize shareholder profits.

How we keep score will be completely different.

The quest will be how to honor God in every act of business. Innovation and creativity will fuel excitement. Time with God will be scheduled, protected, and honored.

I think business is important to God. Jesus spent more than half of his adult life as a carpenter. And that's not insignificant. In fact, it's very significant. Of his thirty-three years on earth, only the last three years were spent in full-time public preaching and teaching. The other thirty years were spent growing up and then being a carpenter—a businessman.

Jesus was involved with learning a trade, selecting raw materials and transforming trees into salable items to help people in their daily lives. He dealt with vendors, quality control, pricing his products, inventory and all the normal aspects of being a businessman, a carpenter in Nazareth.

I believe God loves business and that he wants to be a part of our making a living far more than we've ever grasped. Isn't business about…offer and acceptance? I submit to you that partnership with God is about …offer and acceptance.

So many people have focused completely on the last three years of Jesus' life and ignored all the implications of the reality that most of his earthly life was as a businessman. This has caused many people to think that for them to have any "real" value to God, to make their life count for God, they had to be in "ministry." I don't think this was God's intent.

Jesus said in John 12:50, "…Whatever I say is just what the Father has told me to say." And in John 5:19-20, Jesus said, "I tell you the truth, the Son can do nothing by himself; he can do only what he sees his Father doing, because whatever the Father does the Son also does. For the Father loves the Son and shows him all he does…."

This says that Jesus could do nothing by himself and that he only did what he saw the Father doing. Did these verses of scripture I mention here apply only to his last three years of being on earth?

Surely not. They didn't apply just to his three years of full-time "ministry." They also applied to his life before "ministry." They applied to his life in business as a carpenter. The reason Jesus knew the voice of the Father when he was in "ministry" was that he knew the voice of the Father while he was in business as a carpenter.

God is into business, science, technology, problem-solving, inventions, and every single aspect of all of our daily lives. God is not just in "ministry." God is in the office. God is in the laboratory. God is in your home. God is in every part of our daily lives.

The move of God that many church people talk about is not going to be like the traditional, historical model. I think it's going to take place where we work, how we work, as we work.

3

We will begin to partner with God, and to know him, not just about him, and achieve results never before thought possible.

This move of God will not be at the feet, the hands or from the mouths of the people on any platform. No excellent preachers nor master orators of the Bible will be able to take any credit for what will come to pass. It will not be centered in any city, denomination, sect, or country. It will be a revival of the common man where the common man is.

The common man will take the power of God to the common man. The common man will arise to take their place in the grand scheme of God's panorama, allowing God to move through them in every area of their lives.

Will you be one of them?

You're here at a very good time.

It's not too late....

Chapter 2

A Business Is Born,
or
I Guess I Was Born Into Business

Mom asked Dad, "Frank, how are we going to send these children to college?" Dad didn't have an answer. He was a pastor of a small church and seldom received enough money to live on. So Mom began to cry out to God to show her how to send my sister and me to college.

Mom taught music lessons in our home and one day when she was having her teaching piano tuned, she kept asking the piano tuner where she could buy pianos. Finally, in exasperation, he turned and said, "Mrs. Cottingham, you can go right over to Glasses Warehouse in Walterboro and buy all the pianos you want."

> Mom began to cry out to God to show her how to send my sister and me to college.

That night Mom and Dad made plans to go to Walterboro that weekend. Walterboro was only about fifty miles from our home in Charleston, South Carolina, but back then that trip seemed a whole lot farther than it would today. I still remember getting to Walterboro and stopping at a gas station to ask directions to Glasses.

We found it, a large warehouse building with all kinds of stuff in it. Sure enough, he had some pianos. Mom examined several and finally bought two for $100. We rented an open-top U-Haul trailer, loaded them up, and took them home.

Mom worked and worked on those pianos. She learned to tune them, replace the bridle straps and make all the little adjustments they needed to get them playing well. She then put a little ad in the newspaper and sold them at a profit. We were in business.

You know where we were the next weekend? Right, at Glasses warehouse in Walterboro again. We took a U-Haul with us that time and again came back with two more big upright pianos we bought for $50 each.

She worked them over and sold each of them for $100 and then we were back at Glasses again. Before long, our garage was no longer used for anything but pianos. Mom continued to teach music lessons and sell pianos with help from Dad. The business grew each year.

We bought and sold a lot of pianos and one day a "rep" for a new piano manufacturer called on us. After he talked with us a bit, he offered to sell us six brand new pianos on 90-day terms. That added up to several thousand dollars! That was a mighty big step. My parents prayed and finally said yes. Dad later said that he had decided to say yes if Mom didn't buck him. Mom later said that she had decided to say yes if Dad didn't buck her. They found they were in agreement.

The business continued to grow and some ten years later, we bought the house next door to us and used it entirely for the business. By the time I was a senior in high school, we carried a stock of about twenty new pianos, twenty used pianos, dozens of guitars, accordions, organs and lots more. And it was all paid for. They never took out any loans.

> Prayer, just acknowledging God and talking with him, was just as natural for my parents to do as talking with each other.

Now that would sound like just another neat "growing your own business" story except that as I grew up, over and over again, I would hear my parents praying. They would pray and worship God, pray for our family and loved ones, pray for God's will in our lives, pray for wisdom and direction in the business, pray about ordering more pianos, pray about advertising strategies and sales and all that pertained to the business.

Prayer, just acknowledging God and talking with him, was just as natural for my parents to do as when they talked with each other. There was no distinction between sacred things and making a living. It was all one. They depended on God for wisdom and direction. Did they work hard? You bet, sometimes very long and very hard. But God was a part of all of it.

Many times Mom and Dad would leave a salesman waiting and go into the next room to pray, asking for the direction of the Lord. Did they always get it right? No. Mom often said that when she prayed about making decisions, if she felt the green light, "They were easy to pay for." When she ordered without that green light, "Those were hard to pay for."

The "green light" was her way of saying she had that still, calm peace about what to do. When she had peace, she moved ahead and it was so much better than when she tried to make it happen on her own.

Praying about business and giving it to God was just as natural as praying about family matters and giving ourselves to God. As I grew up, Mom and Dad modeled for me what has become one of the passions of my life—to help merge God and business.

> I remember more than once Mom calling a "family meeting" to ask us kids for input and to talk and pray about the business.

One Wednesday night when I was about ten years old, Mom and Dad had gone to church. I was at the kitchen table fixing a peanut butter and jelly sandwich when all of a sudden, I realized I was not alone. An angel appeared before me. I was totally terrified.

The angel was large, tall, broad-shouldered, all white and oh, so beautiful. His head did not touch the ceiling, nor did his feet touch the floor. He looked at me with great love and said these simple words, "Tell others about Jesus."

He remained there a few moments as I stared at him. His size, beauty and majesty held me in awe. Then he disappeared. When I realized he was gone I jumped up and ran to my sister. She was just finishing a shower when I began banging on the door yelling for her because I was still so very afraid.

Before she could open the door, I heard Mom and Dad entering the house so I ran to them and told them all about this. Mom wrote the account of this in the front of her Bible that night. And I'm so glad she did. I've read it many times.

During my high school years, I began to leave God out of my life. I lived only for myself and did things I thought were exciting. I ended up attending the University of South Carolina majoring in finance. I guess I was fairly atypical because even though my lifestyle not honor God at that time, I still paid my tithes and often knelt down to pray.

One Friday morning at 5:30 A.M. in March, 1974, I suddenly awoke and heard a voice inside me that I recognized as God saying, "Go home." I got up and rode my motorcycle 110 miles from Columbia to our home in Charleston. I walked in and Dad was at our dining room table praying, as was his custom every morning. He smiled and said with so much love, "It is so good to see you." We talked awhile and he suggested we go have breakfast with a pastor friend and a visiting evangelist from Ireland named Leslie Hale.

I was less than excited about meeting with two other preachers, but I agreed. We met them at Shoney's Restaurant where Leslie spoke a lot about the move of God in Ireland. Two hours later we walked outside the restaurant and Leslie Hale said, "I think that we should pray."

So we all joined hands in a little circle, right outside the door of this busy restaurant, at high noon, and began praying. Almost immediately the other three laid their hands on me praying out loud for me. I began to weep and weep. Something in me broke. I felt clean. I felt peace. I felt an awesomeness, a trust.

When I finally opened my eyes, I could see people all around staring at me, but I could not have cared less. For I knew that the power of the Holy Spirit had touched me. The other two men said goodbye and left. Dad and I went to his car and just sat there together as I cried for joy. It was real, so very real.

After graduating from USC, I moved back home and worked in real estate and helped my parents in the music business for a year. My new relationship with God was so exciting and wonderful. I found myself wanting to read the Bible, but it seemed so complicated and I just couldn't enjoy it. I kept looking for something in it I could understand. Then I found the book of Proverbs.

> I found myself wanting to read the Bible but it seemed so complicated. I kept looking for something I could understand. Then, I found the book of Proverbs.

Every night I'd come in and get a glass of milk and start reading Proverbs. I'd read and read and read. I'd often read five to ten chapters a night. More than once, I actually read the whole book of thirty-one chapters in one sitting. It was the only thing that made sense to me at that time. I seemed to drink in those words like water to a thirsty man.

During that year, I began to feel my life was about to change in a major way. I felt it more and more. That feeling increased to the point that, literally, the very first thought I had every single day when I awoke was, I wonder if today I'll know the next step.

In August of 1975, while home for lunch, I saw the back of an Abundant Life magazine published by Oral Roberts that was advertising the opening of the Oral Roberts University Graduate School of Business, offering a masters degree in business administration (MBA). It had a coupon to fill out and send to them for information about their MBA program. I remember thinking that I would love to get my MBA degree some day. I filled out that little coupon and mailed it.

A couple of days later, a man from ORU called and said, "Ted, I just want to ask you if you want to come out here and be a part of the first MBA class that begins in *two weeks.*"

I tell you, tears welled up in my eyes. There was this incredible tingling feeling that started in my toes and came slowly up my legs and up my entire body. I was completely and totally overwhelmed and tears began to run down my face.

I could hardly speak. I finally got out the words, "Uh, uh, uh … YES!"

He then asked me, "Can you pay your way?"

Oh. At that time, all the money I had was three hundred dollars. I asked him to hold on and went into the kitchen and told my parents. Mom straightened up and said, "You go tell them yes. God will provide."

He told me he would express mail me an application and to get it back to him immediately. I hung up the phone. I knew that I knew—that was my direction and God would open that door to ORU.

But before I even left that room to go back into the kitchen, I clearly heard another voice say to me, "Who do you think you are, poor boy? You can't get in that school. And if you do get in, you won't make it. You don't have the brains." This was before I even got back into the kitchen! I quickly realized a spiritual war was on to derail my destiny. I decided to fast until I heard from ORU.

Oral Roberts University did accept me into their MBA program, and yes, God did provide. I know Mom and Dad fasted and prayed often for his help with all the extra expenses, and he did. God sent piano sales and blessed the music business so divinely. Every time I needed to pay my tuition, the money was there.

I could have found work somewhere during my time at ORU, but Mom didn't want me to work. She would tell me, "God has put you there and that's your job. We'll pray in the money. Now you apply yourself 100 percent to that job." So that's what I did.

It was one of the greatest experiences of my life. Not only did ORU open my eyes to the world, excellence, and the Holy Spirit like I'd not known, but it was also the setting where I met my life companion, Barbi Cook, a Southern belle from below Nashville, Tennessee.

I graduated with an MBA degree from Oral Roberts University in 1977, married Barbi, and worked for ORU as assistant to the business manager of the university for a year. ORU then offered me the fantastic opportunity to travel with Rev. Bob DeWeese as the seminar coordinator representing ORU all over the United States. I did this for about two years and loved it.

They then offered me the job of being the business manager of the newly opened ORU Family Medical Clinic. About a year later I was called in, the door shut, and the chairman of the Department of Family Medicine said, "Ted, God is calling you to work somewhere else." Well, it's sure funny now, but it wasn't funny then. And to top it all off, the very last day of my work there, I learned that Barbi was pregnant with our first child, Amy. Wow.

"Ted, God is calling you to work somewhere else."

I didn't think I would have any trouble finding a new job, but every job that appealed to me required more formal accounting education than I had acquired, even though I had my MBA. I began to pray more and more and to seek God about the next step. I applied for so many jobs at the Williams Companies, a major corporation in Tulsa, that they knew me in the personnel department on a first name basis.

After some three months had gone by, I felt pretty desperate. One afternoon it simply struck me to pick up the phone and again call someone in personnel at the Williams Companies. I began to talk with the lady in a pretty passionate manner and the words just didn't quit. I began to tell her that I knew I could do a number of jobs there if I could just be given the opportunity, and that I'd even work a month or more without pay to prove it.

Finally, she interrupted me and so kindly said that she would call me back in a little while. She phoned me in about two hours and said, "Ted, how would you like to be an internal auditor?"

I told her, "That'd be great. I'd love it." Actually, I didn't even know what one was, but I knew it sounded like something in a financial area. I wound up working for the Williams Company for over three years and it was a wonderful experience.

During that time at the Williams Companies I studied like crazy, taking accounting and computer courses in the evenings. In fact, one summer they let me work half time for half pay so I could pick up another four accounting courses. I spent many of my lunch hours in the 48th floor tax library studying everything they had.

I really enjoyed studying about income tax and decided to start doing tax work as a sideline business out of my home. I sent out about fifty postcards announcing my new venture. I did about a dozen tax returns for clients that first year on our dining room table.

The next year I sent out about a hundred post cards and did about twenty-five returns. I was rolling. I really wanted to be in my own business. I was studying all the accounting magazines and books about how to open and run your own accounting business. Barbi and I discussed it often, believing it was right for me to be in business but agreed we should wait until the right time.

In the fall of 1983, my audit manager at the Williams Companies told me that I should expect to start traveling about seventy percent of the time, doing out of town audits. Barbi and I now had two toddlers and I knew being gone from my family like that was just not an option for me. I had a choice and I made it. My family was more important to me than that job.

I resigned and opened my own accounting and tax business one block from our home on Lewis Avenue, a busy four-lane road. The office I rented had three rooms in it and I was able to negotiate with the owner to rent just a small part of it.

In business at last. *But what have I gotten myself into?*

"Many are the plans in a man's heart, but it is the Lord's purpose that prevails" Proverbs 19:21.

Chapter 3

I've Tried So Very Hard—Haven't You?

I had only one account that paid me a very small amount each month when I started, but Barbi and I both knew in our "knower," the depths of our heart, that somehow it really was right. I had a beautiful Karman-Ghia automobile that I sold to purchase my first computer and Dad let me borrow his old truck.

I purchased the accounting software I needed and I was really excited. I was truly in my own business at last. I had dreamed of this many, many times. I studied how to make the software do what I wanted and aside from that, I'd walk and pray, walk and pray, walk and pray.

You know why I walked so much while I prayed don't you? Sure, because otherwise, if I was on my knees, I'd soon go to sleep. So I'd walk and pray out loud. Walk and pray. And eventually, every day, into my mind would drop a name of someone or some group of people to call or write and tell them what I was doing.

> Now, I'd often walk or drive down the street to my new office and wonder what I'd do that day.

One morning while I was praying, the name of a local businessman dropped in my mind to call for lunch. I did and we had lunch that day at the old Argentina Steak House. I still remember it so well because he ordered and ate a huge hot fudge sundae before we got our steak fingers and fries. I told him what all I was doing and he soon said, "You know, our church is looking for an accountant." I met with them and got the account. That church was my second client. I was on my way.

Oh, boy. Work and work and pray and work and pray to get business and then get it and…then…have to do it! Oh, catching them up, doing bank reconciliations, revising their chart of accounts, meeting with them to try to make their financial statements meaningful, etc. I learned real quick, when I was in the office doing the work, I wasn't out there meeting with people getting more work to do. Balancing marketing, sales and production was already a challenge. But it was worth it. I was in my own business and I knew I was where I was supposed to be.

I had an incredible foundation to build on because, as an Internal Auditor with the Williams Companies, I had audited everything from steel fabrication mills, oil pipeline terminals, and rural farm retail outlets to the corporate credit union and executive benefits. Working with various businesses of all kinds and sizes, I began to learn one invaluable lesson after another. Line upon line, precept upon precept, I learned. Day after day, month after month, year after year, I was interfacing with the intimate parts of businesses, both big and small.

> At that time, my only vision was to get and do monthly financial statements for small businesses.
> That was my vision and that's what I got.

I usually wound up working with the owners to get their financial statements to a point where they were comprehensive, meaningful, management information tools that could really help them in their decision making. My objective was never to just compile the numbers on a piece of paper; it was to help these businesses grow.

Several years went by and the clients got bigger. One day a client of mine wanted to hire me full time to install a new computer system with all new accounting software for payroll, general ledger, order entry, inventory, receivables and payables. What an opportunity. I declined to work with them full time but worked out an agreement with them to work half time until Christmas (it was summer then).

After a few weeks, I went in one day to find business cards on my desk with my name on them. The job title underneath my name: Vice President Finance.

Working there half time birthed in me the idea of being a part time business manager for multiple companies. Soon thereafter, a large church with a daycare and school called me. I wound up being their part time business manager, on-site there one day a week. Then sometime later, another large church called me and I did the same with them. Then a very prestigious law firm called me and I wound up there two days a week as their administrator, responsible for everything you can imagine. And I still did consulting with other companies both in Tulsa and some in other states.

One day a friend of mine took me to a Christian men's breakfast. Afterward we were talking about my focus on helping companies grow and get to the next level. At one point he said, "Ted, you're more than just an accountant." I liked that phrase and began using it as my slogan.

It didn't take me long at all to realize that most really good things and clients came to me through friends and through relationships. Even back then, I would jot little notes here and there about how to merge God and business.

I worked hard and my income increased. I worked long hours and applied myself diligently. I tried so hard to pray consistently and operate my business with integrity and honesty and do a good job. But it wasn't easy. It was hard. No matter how much money I made, it was never enough. There never seemed to be quite enough of me to go around.

I tried so hard to do good. I tried so hard to be a good husband, a good dad, a good businessman. I tried so hard. I tried to always be in church and give and do all they wanted. I tried to keep all the rules. I tried to keep a balance between time spent with work and family, but that was always a challenge.

Everywhere I turned it seemed as if people wanted something from me, and no matter what I gave, they always wanted more. I began to wonder if I brought any pleasure to anyone. I wanted so much to bring joy and pleasure to others.

I tried to learn, learn, learn, study, improve, innovate, make more money and keep everybody happy. But it was hard. So many times I cried out to God for help with all these things. Sometimes it seemed like he heard me and helped but often there was nothing.

So many times I felt like I was trying so hard to do right and please everybody. So many times were painful. Enough was never enough. I often felt as if I was beating my head against a brick wall until I was bleeding, and though standing there in a pool of my own blood, I was still trying to please people and do what I thought was expected of me.

Some of those are unpleasant and painful times to recall, but fortunately, pain usually brings change.

I heard Billy Joe Daugherty begin to teach on prayer and encourage everyone to attend what he called "early morning prayer" in a school auditorium from 6:30 A.M. to 7:30 A.M. I heeded the call. I still remember the first time I walked into that room with all those people praying out loud, almost all of them men. I just stood there, shocked. I thought I knew how to pray but these people, wow, they knew how to pray like I'd never heard. And they weren't wimpy about it either.

I didn't know what else to do but start in. I began to pray, but I found myself over and over being so impressed to pray what the leader prayed. I'd never done that before, but it seemed right. So I just prayed exactly what the leader prayed, just a word or two behind him. His prayers became my prayers.

Time after time I went and each time I'd start off this same way, but I'd soon be off on my own track praying. When I ran out of words to pray, I'd again pray what the leader prayed until I was off and running on my own again.

Several years later I heard an evangelist speak about early morning prayer and how God had spoken to him to pray an hour a day. He challenged a group of men one Saturday morning in Tulsa to give God an hour a day for a year to test it. He especially directed this to one of my friends, but I took the challenge.

I decided to really test this early morning prayer deal. I made a commitment to pray consistently, daily, whether I felt like it or not, and whether I felt like God was listening or not. I'd often go and kneel and pray for maybe twenty minutes, then I'd walk and pray for another twenty or so minutes. Often I'd read the Bible for a bit and then go and pray a few minutes for some other person there at prayer.

I went every day for an hour for about five months. It was during this time that my prayer life really began to have life. Since then, early morning prayer has been and is still today, a very integral part of my life.

A few years ago I began to spend time with God while jumping on my son's big trampoline in our backyard. My backyard has become a sanctuary for me. I still often jump and pray, jump and pray, jump and pray. So often God speaks to me while jumping and praying. I almost never go jump without a tablet and pen with me.

After I jump I usually walk around my backyard and pray, sometimes leaping and twirling and dancing around in just simple childlikeness to him. I don't know how David in the Bible danced before the Lord, but I guess I have my own version. My neighbors probably think I'm a nut but that's okay. I've never mentioned it and they haven't either.

Sometimes my relationship with God is awesome, exhilarating and fulfilling, mountaintop experiences. But it has all the normalcy of just regular life as well. And sometimes regular life is hard, disappointing—a good client is lost, a business idea fails, a close friend dies in a car wreck, kids act like kids. Trying to balance life's demands, pay the bills and be all things to everyone is often tough. No rose garden.

But just as Jesus said in John 10:17-18, "…I have authority to lay it [my life] down and authority to take it up again…."— though he was speaking of himself literally, of his physical body—we also have the power to lay our own life down and to raise it up again, in a spiritual sense.

We have the power to lay down our life at the foot of the Cross of Jesus, surrendering all that we are, all that we ever will be, all that we have, and all that we ever will have, and then pick ourselves back up and go walk out our daily lives in him and with him and through him.

I'm calling you today to lay down your life, your skills, abilities, gifts and talents, your past, present, and future, your wisdom, understanding and knowledge—your all, at the foot of the Cross. And when you stand up, stand up in the power of his might.

Who can God use? Those with clean hands and a pure heart. Do you qualify now? Maybe not, but that's okay. He accepts each of us where we are, and becoming more Christ-like is part of the adventure. I'm calling you to the adventure of your life. I can assure you there is nothing like it.

One day I was in our home and I suddenly remembered (or was reminded is more like it) that, in my garage was….

Chapter 4

God, I've Never
Talked With You Like This

One day I was suddenly reminded that in my garage was a big wrench called a pull-handle, and a role of wire that I had kept when I completed my six years of service in the U.S. Air Force Reserve. I knew that I knew, right at that moment, that I had to return it and that I had to acknowledge that I'd kept it, and ask their forgiveness. I had those items probably ten years. I could have easily justified myself or excused myself in some way, but I knew this had come to my attention for a purpose. I had a choice.

> I knew that wire and wrench meant nothing at all to the U.S. Air Force, but it meant something to the will of God in my life. I had a choice.

I'd used so much of that wire that I went and bought another roll like it. I put both rolls in a package with that big pull-handle wrench, wrote a letter telling them what I had done, and that I was sorry, and sent it all back to the U.S. Air Force.

I began to seek God more and more.

Prayer 1—A prayer that changed my life

One day I was jogging around the block, like I do about twice a year. Somehow I began to think about my son, Christopher, and about a specific incident with him when he was a little tyke. One day I had to spank him over something and afterward, after he got his bearings, he walked back up to me. I was standing in our hallway. He put his little arm around my leg, just above my knee (that'll tell you how little he was) and said, "Daddy, thank you for loving me enough to spank me."

21

As I was running down the street, that incident with Christopher seemed to stay with me. I began to think about myself and my relationship with God my father. I began to think about having the same level of trust in God that my little son had in me. I began to wonder if I could say, "Daddy God, thank you for loving me enough to spank me." Thoughts like this had never before entered my mind.

I had always had a pretty healthy fear of God and his wrath and judgment. I kept thinking about all this and whether or not I trusted God enough to really seek his correction. And all of a sudden, as I was running down the street, I spoke this out loud:

"God, please correct me where I'm wrong."

Oh. Tears began to pour down the sides of my face as I ran. Over and over I said to God, "I trust you God, correct me where I'm wrong. I don't want to be a wayward child. I trust you. Correct me, O God." The tears continued. I knew something very significant was happening in my relationship with God.

I began to pray this frequently. And still do. Often. "God, please correct me where I'm wrong. I don't want to be a wayward child. I don't want to be another one that is just 'right in my own eyes.' I want to know you and to please you. Please correct me."

> God, thank you for loving me enough to spank me.

Sometime later, the idea came to me to also pray the prayer, "Lord, discipline me." I have to tell you, once again, I really had to think about it and decide if I *really* meant it. This is not something I took lightly at all. I still remember my trepidation with which I said it that first time. I finally got it out and began to pray, "Lord, discipline me."

And still later, I began to search my heart and ponder whether or not I should pray the prayer, "Lord, judge me." This was the hardest of all. I believed it was right. It seemed almost like he tugged my heart to do it. I finally did it. I began to pray, "Lord judge me. You know me, you know my heart. I trust you. I trust you. I trust you. Correct me, Lord. Discipline me, Lord. Judge me, Lord." I have prayed that so many times. I've now told him these things hundreds, maybe thousands of times. And I meant it. Explicitly. I still do.

I can't say any of this is simple. It isn't. But as I sought the Lord, he made himself known. "I love those who love me, and those who seek me find me" (Proverbs 8:17). "You will seek me and find me when you seek me with all your heart" (Jeremiah 29:13).

Prayer 2—

"Lord, I don't want anything in my life that's not of you."

I began to pray, "Lord, I don't want anything in my life that's not of you. Please take everything out of my life that does not please you or is not of you. That includes feelings, thoughts, emotions, friends, clients and everything else. God, I trust you. I don't want anything in my life that's not of you."

It didn't seem like any direct result came from these prayers at the time I began praying them, but looking back now, I can see the journey. God was re-establishing priorities. There have been many changes in my life in every single one of these areas that I prayed about.

As you start praying these types of prayers, you, too, will find changes come in your life—changes for good. "For I know the plans I have for you, declares the Lord, plans to prosper you and not to harm you, plans to give you hope and a future" (Jeremiah 29:11).

Prayer 3—

Over and over during the last ten years, I have felt like God asked me many times, "What do you want?" I'd talk with him about this and that, but would always end up deferring to him and what he wanted for me. I could do this explicitly because I had come to the point that I trusted him. But still, many times, that question would come from him to me, "What do you want?"

One day I was praying and I again felt like he asked me, "What do you want?" I suddenly blurted out:

"God, please let me do what I'm born for."

And then I added, "Whatever that is Lord, if you want me to be a little accountant on Lewis Avenue in Tulsa the rest of my life, that's okay. If you want me to continue consulting, that's fine. If you want me to preach, that's fine. If you want me to be an employee with some company, that's fine. Whatever you had me born for is what I want."

I was tired of going around the mountain over and over again—that mountain being what I thought I wanted, going after it, asking him to help me in it, and then being unfulfilled in it even if it was achieved.

I came to the realization that his ways are better than my ways, that he loves to surprise me, and that he is not on my timetable.

Caution: Be assured the path to fulfilling God's plan for your life will not be as you suppose. To do what he had you born for, he will have to "uproot, tear down and destroy" the traditions of man that adversely affect your thinking so that he can "build and plant" you. See Jeremiah 1:10.

> I believe he asks all of us this question at some point in our lives: "What do you want?"

Joseph, at age thirty, became the most powerful businessman in history (Genesis 41:39-44), but who would have ever thought that his path to power and achievement would be so circuitous as to include him being falsely accused and spending some thirteen years in prison?

When I began praying this prayer, I had no idea what was in store for me. I began to pray this prayer almost every day and did so in earnest. I began to spend more time in general prayer and Bible study as well. These times became longer and more wonderful. His presence became more and more real to me.

Then as time went on, my large clients began leaving. One major client I'd had for twelve years left. Another very significant one I'd had for several years also left me. This was not at all what I had in mind. I began to feel farther and farther off my map and less and less in control of my destiny.

Although my times with God seemed to get richer and richer, my income steadily went down. "God, what happened to the prosperity message?" I was suspicious. I tried to consciously challenge myself over and over. Was I missing God? Was I deceived? But over and over, I would have times in the presence of God that let me know I was drawing closer to him.

Before my quest to really know God, I had everything paid for except my house. Now with my clients leaving, I soon went through the cash I had and then I went through the credit I had. Believe me, not being able to pay my bills was painful and humiliating. I was not in control. I cried out daily to God for wisdom and help. Except for times in his presence that were so very rich, much of it was no fun. My income dropped to virtually nothing for months.

I wasn't sitting around idle, waiting for things to come to me on a silver platter either. I was sending out resumes, writing letters, and seeking clients. I was doing all I knew to do.

I kept pondering Matthew 6:24 where Jesus was teaching that we cannot serve two masters; we cannot serve God and money. I prayed over and over for him to help me serve him and not money and to give me an understanding of this scripture. I told him I wanted to opt out of the worlds system of money and understand the economy of God.

25

I began to realize how incredibly indoctrinated we are to the worlds system of doing business as opposed to doing business God's way. I began to see how often money motivates our decisions rather than God. I began to see that God wants us to use the spiritual gifts he's given us in business and not just in a church setting.

I began to learn that honesty and integrity in all things, especially the really *little* things, is the foundation for truth to come into our hearts. I would have never guessed that so many important truths would come to me during such a time of pain in other areas of my life.

You may not experience anything like I did. In fact, I'm quite confident your journey in praying to God to help you do what you're born for will not be like mine. You're unique. You are uniquely you. And he will lead you.

Prayer 4— and more

"I want everything you have for me Lord."

After I began praying these other prayers, it came to me one day to pray for what I wanted in the place of some things that seemed to be taken out. I began to pray, "I want everything you have for me, Lord. Whatever it is, whatever it looks like. I am not ashamed of the gospel of Jesus Christ."

More prayers I began to consistently pray were...

"God, make what's important to you important to me, and make what's unimportant to you unimportant to me."

"I want to please you. Lord, help me please you. Please help me please you."

"Lord, let me see my blind spots."

"Let me know your heart, your thoughts, your ways."

"More of you, Lord. More of you, God. More of you, Jesus. More of you, Holy Spirit. More Lord, more Lord."

"Increase my capacity to receive from you, Lord."

I began to pray more and more scriptures. I went and bought several books that have scriptures paraphrased into prayers and began praying them. Oh, how powerful this is.

One of my favorite scriptures to pray was, "Let the words of my mouth and the meditations of my heart be acceptable to you, O Lord my strength and my redeemer" (Psalm 19:14 KJV).

Other prayers I began praying diligently included…
"Open my eyes, open my ears."

"Lord, here I am. I'm all yours."

"Lord, open my eyes to the things of your Spirit. Open my eyes to see you, to see what you want and see how to do what you want. Open my ears that I may hear your voice and always know your voice. I trust you."

"Here I am."

"Teach me and teach me to teach."

"Draw our family closer together and closer to you."

"Teach me to talk, O God."

"Teach me your ways."

Many times I would pray a prayer that seemed to just come out of my heart, somehow bypassing my mind altogether. One day, one such prayer was: "God, please don't promote me beyond my character."

"You know what I can handle and what I can't. I don't want to disappoint you, Lord. I used to think I could handle so much. I used to think I could handle anything. Now, I know better. I have been transparent with you God and really, I don't know what the future holds. So Lord, protect me from myself. Whatever my future holds, don't promote me beyond what my character can handle."

This adventure was getting more adventurous all the time. I felt I was so far off my map, out of my own control, that sometimes I felt suspended between heaven and earth.

I had always known somehow, down deep in my heart, that there was more of God available to me than I had ever experienced. I was finally experiencing it. And it was worth it all.

> "God, please don't promote me beyond my character."

The adventure of discovering the depth of the beauty of his presence became richer and richer. The more I came to know him, the more I realized there is to know. How awesome. It was no longer just hope or theory or desire. He was real.

There's another whole realm. No, there are realms and realms that God has prepared for those who choose to know him.

When I cried out to God, "Correct me where I'm wrong," I started a journey. I had made a decision, unknowingly, to mature. I didn't even think of it that way at the time, but...

I was moving into... un-charted waters. Then....

Chapter 5

God, You've Never
Talked With Me Like This Before

One day I was sitting at my desk just working away when all of a sudden I felt God speak to me so clearly these words:

"You don't value my words."

I was astonished. I was shocked actually. My jaw dropped open, literally. I laid down my pen, slid back my chair and just pondered that thought. I knew that was the voice of God to me, but I thought I placed a super high value on his words already.

Over the years, I often took the time and effort to get a scrap of paper to jot down the thoughts that came to me that I believed were from God. Some of them actually found their way into a manila file folder in the garage. But obviously, God didn't think much of the way I was doing it. So I now had this dilemma: how to respond.

I pondered and prayed about this for weeks. I knew that, regardless of what value I thought I placed on what I believed were God's words to me, my actions in dealing with them did not please him.

> For God to speak to me about valuing his words more, it was important to him. Therefore, they had to become more important to me.

Although I kept asking him how he wanted me to respond, he never told me. I finally decided that I had to do something. I couldn't ignore this. It was on my mind enough that a few weeks later I did all I could think of to show more value to those words.

I finally bought a full-sized three-ring notebook, filled it with paper just like my kids use in school, and began to carry it with

29

me everywhere I went. It had more than adequate space for me to record whatever thought I felt like he was giving me. This was a big change for me. But I was resolved to do whatever it took.

I've changed the kind of notebook I carry several times over the last few years, but I'm almost never without it or a tablet of some kind. I keep these full-sized tablets beside my bed, in each car and make sure I never run out of them.

I've written note after note on a multitude of topics until now I've filled over ten notebooks and two cardboard boxes. I've had to organize and reorganize how I keep track of what he gives me numerous times.

But now, I am referencing some of those notes as I write this book. I realize I have so much more written down than I can ever put into one book. Would you believe that one of my greatest problems in writing this book was not what to put in it but what to leave out for now and use later?

Now why is this so important? Because what we do with what we have always determines our next step.

> What we do with what he gives us and how we respond to it determines the flow of future words to us.

It's just like with my teenage son, Christopher. If I ask him to get three things done today and he doesn't take the time to jot them down and only remembers to do one of the three things, when I get home, I'm not thrilled with his accomplishments for the day.

And if that happens several times, it doesn't take long for me to realize that my requests to him are not real important to him. But when I mention several things to him and he grabs a pen and records them and gets them done in a timely manner, I know he's valuing my words and requests. They're important to him.

Then I get to where I know I can trust him more and more with things of greater importance and complexity.

So it is with God speaking to us, I believe. The more value we place on the words we receive from him, the more careful we will be to record them in a notebook that we reference often and document for others. The more we value them and put them into practice, the more he'll give us.

So I recommend to you, increase the value you place on the words God gives you. Whether those words are for you individually, your business, your children, or whatever, record them, document them and value them. Revisit them often. Ponder them. Ask God about them. Do what he tells you to do.

I believe God has spoken to many of us numerous times when we have not valued it. There have been times when he spoke to me in the car while driving, and it was so profound to me that I thought I'd remember it the rest of my life, only to get home a few minutes later and not be able to remember it.

Had I not responded like I did to that phrase several years ago, "You don't value my words," I probably wouldn't be writing this book right now.

What has he said to you? Do you value his words to you? Do you have a specific system of recording and valuing and referencing what he shares with you? If not, please begin to value his words to you more and you will receive more.

Again, one day, working away at my desk in my office, I felt the voice of the Lord say to me:

"You don't value my Word."

Oh, my. Once again I was surprised. Not shocked as much as I was with the one I discussed above, but definitely surprised. So now he tells me I don't value his Word. Well, it was true that I didn't value it enough. Although I had spent much time in it and read many of its books many times, I never had a long-term systematic plan for going through the Bible.

I didn't spend time in it every day. I sure didn't memorize it like some people have done. I'm still not at the place I'd like to be but I've taken steps to spend more time in his Word and give it a higher place in my life. The more I value his Word and give it a high priority in my life, the more wisdom and revelation comes to me through it.

> You want to partner with the living God? You've got to know his Word. Cultivate a love for his Word.

Some months ago the idea of listening to the Bible on cassette tape in my car came to me, and came to me, and came to me. So I purchased a set of Bible tapes and made a commitment that whenever I'm driving, I'd listen to them. I truly had no idea that listening daily to these tapes of God's Word would so further transform my life. Oh, that I had done this when I first came to Christ while I was still in college.

I have always thought that nothing can take the place of reading God's Word. Now, I also believe there's nothing that can take the place of just hearing it.

Both are so powerful. One is as powerful as the other. Both complement and strengthen the other. Over and over, I hear parts of verses I've never understood before and find myself connecting scriptures and having insight as he teaches me in the most precious ways. I've often pulled my car off to the side of the road to grab my pen and tablet to jot down the ideas, notes and wisdom that he gives me as I listen to his Word being read to me.

In addition to reading and listening to his Word more, he has begun to deal with me about reading it out loud. There's something about this vocal declaration of his Word that's more powerful than we think. There's nothing like it.

God's Word is, in fact, a word picture of himself that he's given us to know him, his values, his thoughts and his ways. It is a picture of his love, his mercy, his grace, his judgment and the things yet to come.

At one point Jesus answered a Pharisee's question with, "You have no room [in your heart] for my word" (John 8:37). Don't let him say that about you. Make room for his Word and his ways and his voice. Begin anew.

The wisdom of God is in the Bible, but little of it is on the surface. It has to be mined with the help of the Holy Spirit. The

> The closer we get to God, the more we will love and value his Word.

closer we get to God, the more we will love and value his Word.

I know when we get to heaven we will be shocked to learn what all he revealed to us in his Word that we never saw or understood, or took the time to mine. The true genius of the Godhead is in the Bible.

I don't know that I ever thought of being able to coast a bit, but I was just getting a little comfortable with those things mentioned above when he did it to me again.

God spoke so tenderly to me one day, as I sat working at my desk in my office and said,

"You don't value your word."

I was pierced. Shocked to the tenth degree. My parents taught me honesty and I thought I placed a very high value on my word. I couldn't imagine where this came from. I wanted to say, "Lord, I think you're wrong on this one."

But, once again, I began to ponder and pray about this. I began to ask the Lord often, "Lord, how is this so? How do I not value my word? What should I be doing differently? Lord, please show me, correct me please." Over and over I'd pray like this.

His very timely, kind, insightful response: nothing. Not a thing. Weeks went by. Nothing.

Then one day it came to me that I had made a pledge to a church and I had not paid it off. I'd paid part of it. But oh! That was years ago. *Years* ago. That was over ten years ago. But that thought came to me enough times that I decided it was the Lord letting me know that I had to fulfill my word dealing with that pledge.

One day it came to me that I had made a pledge to a non-profit group of $2,000 and I had only paid $1,000. And yep, once again I couldn't shake the thought and realized I had to make it right. And that pledge, too, was made years ago—maybe fifteen years ago.

Now I began to really think about this kind of thing. "Lord, is this what you're talking about? Pledges I've made in the past? But God, they were called 'faith pledges.'" We were told, "If the money doesn't come in for you to pay this, you're not obligated. You're doing this in faith." That label didn't seem to matter to God in my case. I was to fulfill my commitments and pledges and keep my word.

I wish I could tell you it stopped with just those two. It didn't. Over some months there were some half dozen pledges that I realized I'd paid on in years past that were never fulfilled. I wound up writing all of them and acknowledging my pledge and told them I would work to complete it. Then I began to make payments on them, chipping away at them to get them paid.

All of a sudden, I realized one day—my word was much, much more important than I had ever realized. My word was much more important to God than it was to me! It didn't stop there.

Another time it came to me that, several years before, I had done some work for a man and had charged him more than I should have because I had anticipated that I would have a few more meetings on his project. Those additional meetings never came about and I had forgotten all about it. So I called him to let him know these details and make it right.

Sometime later, it came to me that many years ago, not long after I began my own business, I had done a project for a man that I was not qualified to do. I had done inferior work for him and he let me know it. But he paid me for it. Well, the Lord let me know that this had been a stumbling block to this man. He knew I was a Christian and had dealt with him poorly.

> I had done inferior work for him…. The Lord let me know that this had been a stumbling block to him.

Actually, at the time, it didn't cross my mind to refund his money. I guess I felt like that was his problem. I went on my way. But with the way God was dealing with me about the integrity of my word, I knew I was to write that man, apologize to him and refund his money.

I wrote him and told him why I was writing the letter. I acknowledged that I had done inferior work for him and that God had let me know I had not treated him right and that I was now trying to make it right. I couldn't pay the whole amount at one time but I promised to consistently chip away at it until I got it all repaid. And I did.

God began to deal with me about integrity in all the areas of my life, both large and small, business and family. He let me know that if my wife or one of my kids called me at the office and I told them I'd be home at six o'clock, I should make my word good with them, just as if I'd made that appointment with another businessman who was paying me to meet him. My word to them had to be good, reliable, and trustworthy.

I began to, at the strangest times and places, suddenly remember that I had a book on my shelf that someone had loaned me. I'm sure I'd told them I'd return it, but I hadn't done it. I'd go find it and take it or mail it to them. I came across several cassette tapes that others had loaned me that I returned.

I was learning some big lessons. God cares a whole lot more about these little things than I ever knew or imagined. Integrity in all communications, e.g. accounting, taxes, dating of documents and signatures, punctuality for meetings, appointments, returning things borrowed, etc., are important to him. Very, very important.

My word was much more important to my relationship with God than I had ever realized or comprehended. Just the simple act of keeping my word—doing what I said I would do, when I said I would do it—was part of the foundation of being able to have relationship with him. This was true even if later I didn't want to do it, or it was to my disadvantage to do it.

> We so often have our eyes on doing something big for God and he's just waiting on us to mature to the point we can keep our word and operate in simple integrity.

I began to realize that God was dealing with me about the things that stood between me and what he wanted to do with me. I began to realize that so often we have our eyes on doing big things for God, and he's just waiting for us to mature to the point we can keep our word and operate in simple integrity.

It matters to God how we live. It matters to him what we say and how we fulfill our word. I believe the lack of integrity in small things is what holds so many of us back from fulfilling what's in our heart.

We like to think of ourselves as college graduates, when really, in many areas of our lives, we're still in grammar school.

Do you value your word?

Are you keeping your word—

- To your wife or husband?
- To your kids?
- To the people that can do absolutely nothing for you?
- To your friends?
- To your employees?
- To your employer?
- To your vendors?
- To your customers?
- To God?

Have you made pledges or contracts you didn't fulfill?

Have words of prophecy been given over you that you felt were from God? Did you write them down, visit them often, ask God about them? They may be God's will, God's desire, but you still have lots of choices in the matter. Prophecy often is fulfilled through prayer. And it is pretty hard to pray about things you don't remember.

Do you value His Word? Do you incline your heart to it? Read it? Ponder it? The more you do, the more he will speak to you through it.

I had absolutely no idea where it would take me when I began praying about—

- doing what I was born for,
- asking God to correct me where I was wrong,
- making what is important to him important to me, and
- removing anything in my life not of him.

But I knew his presence was flourishing in my life. I was no longer just learning "about" God. I was experiencing his leading and presence in ways not known to me before.

I know my character was being transformed and my priorities re-established. I knew I was beginning to know not only a whole lot more about God, but I was truly getting to know him. My quest was to know him. And you know what? I think he truly gets excited about people who set their hearts to know him.

And all the while all these writings about God in business continued to come, almost daily, sometimes pages and pages a day.

Then one day while I praying, God spoke to me these simple words…

"Motive is more important than attitude."

Chapter 6

Motive Is More Important Than Attitude

When he said, "Motive is more important than attitude," I didn't know it would change my life. I sensed it was revelation and had significance, but I didn't understand it. I pondered it often. I began to understand that we're not very truthful with ourselves in a lot of areas, especially when we start examining our motives.

Not long ago my wife was so sick that she spent the day in bed. That's really rare for her. While praying for her, I felt God ask me, "Why are you praying for her healing, because you don't want to have to do her work today (meals, errands, etc.)?" I was dumbfounded. My jaw dropped open.

Of course, I shouldn't have been surprised. God had dealt with me about so many other things in my life. If you had asked me ten years ago if my life was clean and my motives pure, I'm sure I would have answered yes. But, as you'll see, he's concerned about a lot of things I had never even thought registered with him.

I'm learning that, to really partner with God, our motives must be pure. And for that to happen, we must lay down our skills, abilities, gifts and talents at the foot of the Cross. But how do we do that? You can say the words but it's a spirit thing, a heart thing, a motive thing. This has to come from within your spirit and your heart.

When you get up from laying down your life at the feet of Jesus, you look the same, you have the same skills, abilities, gifts and talents, but now, you have a different motive.

You'll still work hard, apply yourself diligently, pursue learning and excellence, but it will no longer be just for you. Neither will you be doing it "for God," as if to pay your dues, or meet the expectations of man.

You'll still be you, but your motive will be to please the Master. He'll speak and you'll listen. You'll speak and he'll listen. And communion will occur. Your life will take on new meaning.

Your motive to do, your motive to be, changes. Your motive to honor God in all that you do increases. Your desire to hear his voice and obey increases. Your awareness of the reality of his presence increases to the point that, at times, it's almost tangible.

> Why we do and say things become as important as what we do and say.

In fact, there are times that you'll realize his presence is *more* real than anything else that exists. You begin to want to do all that you do *with* him. You want him to be a part of everything you do. And you start involving him, talking with him, consulting with him in every area of your life. Friendship with God becomes a reality.

Your own self-centeredness begins to decrease. Why we do things start to become as important as what we do. More and more, what comes out of our lives will be love, joy, peace, patience, kindness, goodness, faithfulness, gentleness and self-control. Integrity in small things will begin to have an increasing importance to us.

We begin to realize that everything we do affects our relationship with God. Everything we do, and why we do it, has a result in the physical world and a result in the spirit realm.

I can go to work tomorrow and work just in the natural for me, for money, and for my gratification. I can be totally focused on me, just me, my agenda and what advances and pleases me. Or I can go do the very same work, but do it as unto God, and the result, and the reward, is far different. It becomes synergistic with God.

40

There are many people who wonder why they can't hear God's voice or feel his presence. They wonder why, why, why. "Why don't you speak to me God?" "Why aren't you using me God?" And yet, the things they do alone or in secret, or at work, or with their money, if made public would bring them embarrassment and shame.

Operate in all things with honor and integrity so that if all of your life's details are made totally public, you won't be embarrassed. Because there is nothing hidden. Not really. There's no such thing as really hiding anything. It's just a matter of time until there's "open disclosure" of all that you are and all that you do.

Never, ever usurp authority given another to promote yourself. When you operate in a self-serving manner, cheat on your taxes, communicate half-truths, and live out any part of your life without absolute integrity, it costs you. Oh, you

> "The day will surely come when at God's command Jesus Christ will judge the secret lives of everyone, their inmost thoughts and motives; this is all part of God's great plan, which I proclaim" Romans 2:16 TLB.

may think you get away with it for years, but it hurts your spirit. It injures your spirit and diminishes and delays what God can do with you and in your life.

If you disparage your boss and those in authority, scorn them with contempt and undermine them, you are building your own gallows for yourself, just as Haman did when he had gallows built for Mordecai. See Esther 7:9. When you maneuver to protect your own agenda, your own salary, your budget or department—that which benefits you somehow—at the expense of the company and without the full disclosure and blessings of those in authority, you may advance yourself in the physical realm, but you'll be regressing in your relationship with God.

If you get into pornography, lying, gambling, greed, stealing and the like, you not only begin to decrease your ability to hear the voice of God, but you're also providing a pathway for the very

41

same thing to happen with the others in your home. These things will begin to destroy your communion with God, your spouse, your children, and ultimately—they can destroy you.

One day I was praying and God spoke to me and said, "Motive smells." He has reminded me of this a number of times. In the spirit world, our motives smell. When our motives are self-serving, they stink before God.

More than once I've had someone call me and take me to lunch only to be less than thrilled when, near the end of our lunch, they pull out their sales presentation data. Then I realized, they didn't care about me. They didn't want to spend time with me. They didn't call me out of friendship. They wanted my money, just my money. And they weren't even up front about it. It's a great way to ruin a great meal.

Choose to mature. You have to choose. And don't think that maturity comes with age. That's a myth. There are a lot of immature people walking around today in adult bodies. They look like adults. They're old enough to be adults, some with children and grandchildren, but they've never made some of the seemingly hard choices to grow up.

Do everything you do as unto God and not as unto man.

What is it that has kept us from realizing our potential? Our lack of pure motives must surely be part of it.

Why have our motives been wrong?

We don't know the Scripture nor the power of God. That's the answer Jesus gave the Pharisees in Matthew 22:29 and I believe the very same message is applicable to us today.

I think so often we look for the spectacular that we fail to see the forest for the trees. We fail to see the hand of God at work in our lives and businesses because we're seeking that "really big deal," that "big break" that will "make us."

If we come to God for what he can do for us, rather than because of who he is, and we seek his presents rather than his presence, we will always be disappointed. As long as we seek the spectacular, we will be going in circles in the desert.

As our motive becomes more and more to know him for who he is and not just for what he can do for us, our lives will be transformed and our relationship with him will become an adventure that brings excitement and fulfillment into every single day.

If you want revelation, you can have it. You can go to God and get it. You can have all of God you want. Motive is key. Motive is of paramount importance in the economy of God.

As our motive changes from being self-centered to being God-centered, we'll find ...

...there's another whole realm to operate in.

"...Serve him with wholehearted devotion and with a willing mind, for the LORD searches every heart and understands every motive behind the thoughts" 1 Chronicles 28:9.

Chapter 7

There's Another Whole Realm to Operate In

There's another whole realm to operate in. It's a realm available to every one of us who choose to partner with God.

It's a realm where the Holy Spirit becomes our teacher. Our perspective begins to change from the temporal to the eternal. Our vision enlarges. It's a realm where he is no longer a God far off somewhere, but one who walks with us (Luke 24:32).

It's a realm where the walls start coming down between the sacred and the secular. We begin to realize that all God gave us, all Jesus taught, and all that the Holy Spirit has for us is given to us for every single aspect of our lives, not just for "church" or "ministry."

There's another whole realm where we operate *in* the world, but not of it. We begin to operate with a different motive than the rest of the world and with a different set of values.

It's a realm where we are proactive and diligently pursuing excellence, doing what we can do, but not doing so alone.

It's a realm where the ordinary, daily life of our short term existence merges with the eternal God in a perspective that baffles the normal intellect. Through the blood of Jesus at the cross at Calvary, the way was made for us to experience

> It's a realm understood only by those who choose to respond to the revelation of God's desire for true partnership with us.

his love, his power, his partnership, and his ways that are higher than ours.

It's a realm understood only by those who choose to respond to the revelation of God's desire for true partnership with us.

We become more and more sensitive to the things that affect our relationship with God. Things that affect our spirit like music, what we look at, hear and read, are recognized for the effect they have on us. We become more selective. We become thirsty to feed that which is in us that desires to know the living God. We set our affections on things above rather than things on earth.

It's a realm where we not only have accepted him as our Lord and Savior and pray to him, which is where we all start, but it's where we don't limit him. We begin to grasp his unlimited-ness and believe in more than ourselves and what we physically see. We start to realize that we are not always limited by the natural circumstances around us that may seem insurmountable

We as human beings are so finite. We think in terms of what we see, what we know we can do, and what we can control. That's why we are, by nature, protectionists of our turf, our department and all of our little areas. That's why it's so easy to walk around so conceited and deceived thinking we're someone important in our little world, our company or our church.

This is a realm where we are constantly looking and seeing God's involvement in the daily affairs of our life. It's where he speaks and we listen. It's where we speak and we know he's listening. It's where we sometimes just know things, where he's given us insight beyond the normal and the visible.

I want you to capture another whole mindset that will allow you to go from where you are to all that God has for you. I want you to partner with the Holy Spirit of God because, that's the only way you'll be truly fulfilled in your quest for achievement and significance.

If you leave him out, or give him place as an appendage to what you're doing, let me assure you, regardless of what you do, achieve, or attain, enough will never be enough. It will never satisfy. You will want more and more and it will satisfy less and less.

As we mature in him, we allow him to do things through us and with us that transcend our own natural skills and what we can achieve on our own.

We lack wisdom. We don't lack talent, skills, abilities, or information. We lack wisdom for our next step. We need the Holy Spirit to be our teacher.

When I talk with Christians who say they operate a Christian business, I often ask them what they mean. The response is usually a form of, "Well, we operate by scriptural principles." I then ask what those principles are.

No one ever expects that question. Invariably, they look at me in pause mode and say something like, "Well, we give to missions," or something vague. Bless their hearts, I have yet for more than a couple of people to give me any substantive answer to that question.

I wonder what makes us think we are operating by Biblical principles? Do we have the values and attitudes in our work that God has given us in his Word?

Why do we always talk about scriptural principles? Because principles provide predictability. And we want things to be predictable. We don't often want to march off our map into un-charted waters, do we?

I'm afraid most of us are more interested in the Biblical principles of financial prosperity than in discovering the ones that give us wisdom and insight into what he considers ethical, moral and righteous.

I'm not sure any of us operate by more than a few Biblical principles, much less by true partnership with him. But we will. There's so much more. He has so much more. Let's go after it.

We are the sons of God. I believe God wishes to put sandals on our feet, a robe on our back, a ring on our finger and invite us into his realm. Most of us have stopped at our lowest point, barely crossing the threshold of salvation, never realizing he's asking us constantly to come and dine with him and experience his realm.

As we seek to know and partner with the Holy Spirit we begin to understand that, "...the Spirit gives life," as it says in 2 Corinthians 3:6.

Partnering with the Holy Spirit builds upon Biblical principles and brings them alive.

The following illustrates the difference between attempting to live by Biblical principles in merely our own natural ability and living in dependence on and in partnership with the Holy Spirit:

Biblical principles:	Partnering with Holy Spirit:
Rules	Relationship
Static	Dynamic
Logical	Surpasses logic
Flesh	Spirit
Word of God	Power of God
May be faith driven	Has to be faith driven
Easy to be works driven	Obedience driven
Can practice without knowing God, many do	Have only by knowing God
Can do at will	Can do at His will
You have a map	You're off your map
You're in control	He's in control

Many people will try to operate by scriptural principles who will never begin to partner with Holy Spirit because they will not give up control.

But look at this list; study it. Write down your own list.

48

See, this is where the adventure begins. When you've been diligent but are now off your map—out of control—your security, as you have known it, is vulnerable. You feel secure as long as you feel you're in control, but you realize now you're not controlling everything. You're becoming more and more dependent on God.

Partnership is taking place.

I have wanted to give my people so many things,
   but they couldn't receive them.

They who know who I am-
They've seen themselves as grasshoppers-
Little even in their own sight-
With the ability to accomplish only so very little.

How long have I yearned to gather them under my wing,
as a mother hen her chicks, and nurture them for growth
and development to accomplish what I have for them—
That which I'm giving out-
So they'll embrace me and my ways and wisdom.

If only- If only-
      If only they would allow me to speak to them.

If only they would sit at my feet and let me give them
the experience of being under my wing.

If only- If only they would come and sit at my feet.

If only-
   If only they would ask me about those things that
they only went to the world to try to do and achieve.

If only- If only- If only-

            —They knew me.

Chapter 8

If My Dream Is God-Given,
Why Is It So Hard to Pursue It?

Do you have a dream down deep within your heart? Has it been with you a long time? Do you think your dream could be from God?

You know there's a next step. You probably also know that it won't be automatic. It won't just happen, coming to you on a silver platter. Yet no matter how convinced you might be that it is God's will for you, or that it's a part of your destiny, you realize just dreaming about it won't bring it about.

I suspect you know that some things must happen in your heart for your dream to come about, just like you know that some things must change in your natural circumstances for it to come about. But, "What things must change?" is the question we all face.

> You probably also know that this next step for you will not be automatic. It won't "just happen."

That's what this book is all about.

My teenage son, Christopher, is brilliant, and you know I'm not prejudiced at all. He is so very mature and smart in so many areas that we simply expect him to be that mature and smart in every area of his life...all the time. When he suddenly acts his age, we're often surprised but may not even realize why at the moment.

Our expectations tend to run at the highest level. It is pretty important to recognize this though, to know how to deal with him when he acts like a regular teenager. This is pretty easy for all of us to recognize in someone else, but it's so difficult to recognize that we adults are exactly the same.

We all have areas of our lives that we're more mature in than others. Some of us are pretty mature in a few areas. Most of us are really immature in most areas. You know why? We've not been taught to choose maturity. We thought it came with age and that just isn't true.

The trials and tribulations we face change us. All through them, we make choices that forge our character and make us able to handle the forces we encounter in our quest to partner with God.

No man can face our trials and hard times for us. Else we fail to be strengthened by them. We then have to repeat them and go around and around that mountain again, until we learn to take responsibility for our own actions, whatever the consequences, and choose to mature from them.

> Much of what we blame on the devil "attacking us" is God testing us, trying to grow us up and get us out of diapers. Some of it, I think, is just life.

It says in Hebrews 5:8 (TLB) that, "And even though Jesus was God's Son, he had to learn from experience what it was like to obey when obeying meant suffering." If Jesus suffered, won't we? Look at that verse closely. Notice the phrase, "...When obeying meant suffering." It's easy to obey when it brings us comfort and *things* we want. We seem to never discuss the fact that sometimes, obedience will bring us suffering. And we will never, ever mature until we learn that and choose to obey anyway.

Life comes and trials come and we are to grow and mature, not point the finger of blame and flee responsibility and rebuke situations that we've behaved ourselves into.

Are we kids or adults in our walk with God? Are we into the milk of God's Word or the meat? Or do we even know the difference? Do we understand his voice, his gifts? Do we have twenty years of experience as a Christian, or one year of experience twenty times?

Most people won't take responsibility for their actions or their past, present or future. Most people won't be accountable. Most people won't make the decision to mature. Most won't develop their natural gifts. Most won't develop their spiritual gifts. Most won't learn to really communicate nor how to give and receive counsel and allow others to be free. Most won't give up their control.

> Do we have 20 years of experience as a Christian, or one year of experience 20 times?

Result? They will always be wondering why they could never do what they felt God wanted them to do. Many of them will tell you that they're just waiting on God.

But I assure you, God is looking everywhere for people he can pour himself into, people that will listen to him, people he can impart himself into and give them his creative abilities. Will you choose to be one of them?

You must choose how you deal with your own trials and opportunities and fight to develop your dream and destiny.

Else—
- You'll never grow up.
- You'll always be disappointed.
- You'll always be blaming the "system."
- You'll always be blaming someone else.
- You'll always be wondering why "it" didn't happen.
- You'll always be trying to exercise your "rights."
- You'll never reach your destiny.

Why do trials come? To mature you—so that afterward, (and even during the times that the heavens seem as brass) you still know God is there with you. Isn't that a part of what faith is?

And once through it, you realize he sustained you all the way. He seldom walks with us through things like we think we want him to, but he let's us know he is with us. He will never leave us nor forsake us.

Having come through things we don't like or understand, we still affirm our faith in him. We choose to believe in him and we choose to grow up.

Until you can handle what you don't want to do, with God at the core of your life, with pure motives, you probably won't get to where you want to go.

> Until you can handle what you don't want to do, with pure motives and God at the core of your life, you probably won't get to where you want to go.

During the last five years, I have had many wonderful mountaintop experiences with him, and sometimes I didn't even want to go on living. Truly. At times I felt like all I wanted to do was drop out, go get a cabin in the woods and hide. But, over and over I'd come to God.

As I learn to totally open up before him, I experience his tender presence in ways more precious than I have words to describe. You, too, must learn this to partner with God. Your way will be unique, just as you are unique.

The adventure is before you—

This is a wake-up call to mature.
- Know him; know what he wants,
- Know his voice.
- Use what he has given you and grow.
- Go after your destiny, your dream.

Many will not. Why? Because of wrong thinking. Because of myths held as truth in their minds. For many, the next step will never become clear. They'll continue to do pretty much what they have always done—always wanting more but resigned that they can't do it, they can't reach it.

Many will say something like, "Oh, I don't know. Maybe it's just God's will that I keep doing what I'm doing. Who am I to think I can do such and such?" And of course, at times we all deal with the concept embodied in the phrase, "Who am I to do this thing? Who am I? Little ole me? I'm just a little guy...."

Many will continue to maintain their current habit of wasting hours each day in front of their television, sitting dumb as a sheep and getting dumber, forfeiting the adventure of their lives. They will take on the values of what they see, never choosing to explore the depths of the riches of his glory, of his Word, or experience what they were born to do. Please don't forfeit the fulfillment of your destiny at the altar of a television or a computer.

Ask people why they're not doing what's in their heart and what comes out of their mouths? The answers I hear most often are, "I don't have the money and I have no one to help me."

If we had all the money and people we needed to accomplish our dream, we wouldn't need God, would we? We'd have the power to get it done without him. But I don't think he wants us to do it without him. That's his idea isn't it, to plant something within each one of us that is doable, but not doable alone? It's doable only with him.

> "I don't have the money." "I don't have anyone to help me." We dismiss so easily the dream in our heart because of these "giants" in our way.

Oh, we can do it without him to some extent, sometimes. We can simply look at the way it's being done now and copy it. There are some that are tenacious enough to make lots of things happen. But it is so much more creative, fulfilling and complete

55

when he is at the core of it, and our motive is obedience rather than personal achievement.

Our family was at Silver Dollar City a couple years ago, (our favorite family vacation spot), and I bought a little granite rock that has a saying inscribed in it that is so powerful. It says, "The smallest deed is bigger than the greatest intention." We all have great intentions, but are we taking action to position ourselves so that we really can partner with God?

During my time as in internal auditor for the Williams Companies in Tulsa, I overheard a man talking with a woman one day in the snack bar. The man was apparently a tennis coach and the woman his student. He told her that if she was going to improve her tennis game, she needed to schedule some tennis matches with other people. Her response was, "Oh no, I could never do that. I could never play in front of someone else. I'd be embarrassed. All I ever want to do is just take lessons."

> God is into process—
> growing us up and
> maturing our character.

You may say you're waiting on God, but what if he's waiting on you? I don't want you "just taking lessons" forever. I often think this is exactly where many Christians are, "just taking lessons." There's a time to put legs under your prayers. There's a time to move forward. Over and over in the Bible, we have a picture of God speaking to people, but once they heard, they had to act on that word.

You might find it interesting that in the last year, I've had three completely different dreams that were unmistakable in their message to me: "Get that book done."

I battled the clock, schedules, interruptions, and all sorts of giants to make it a reality. You will too. You'll have to fight to complete your dream. Spiritual forces may come against those who dare to step into their promised land and exercise their rightful birthright to partner with the living God. You have to be tenacious.

Matthew 11:12 says, "From the days of John the Baptist until now, the kingdom of heaven has been forcefully advancing, and forceful men lay hold of it."

Remember the story of the spies who saw the promised land but reported in Numbers 13:33 that, "We seemed like grasshoppers in our own eyes and we looked the same to them."

I know that the grasshopper complex has been the topic of orators for ages. But it's so interesting to me when God speaks to me so clearly about something that I've known before or heard before. One of these times this happened I was in church on a Sunday night during an extended prayer time. As I was walking near the altar, I felt God say to me, "My people see themselves as grasshoppers." You will have to fight to overcome the thoughts that put you down.

There will be seasons of struggle and seasons of harvest. Don't let the seasons of struggle snuff you out. And don't let the seasons of harvest corrupt you.

> The closer you get to where you think you should be, the harder it will be to be humble.

I want you to pierce the veil that has held you back, by the power of the Holy Spirit of God, one step at a time. Sometimes that will be baby step by baby step. Sometimes you'll wonder if you're progressing or regressing, but don't give up. Keep moving toward God and whatever he's told you.

We must be careful not to fall in love with our dream. This at times is so very hard. It's our dream. Our dream becomes our baby and we love our baby. It is ours. We've dreamed it, we've pondered it, we've prayed about it, we've written it down and refined it during hundreds of hours. But you know what? It's not ours. It's his.

Fall in love with your dream and you'll lose your compass. You'll start to lose your sense of balance. You'll lose your ability to be objective and evaluate options, alternatives and direction with patience, counsel and wisdom. Your heart will pound with the reality that you can make it happen; it's your destiny, your calling, and you can do it, you will do it.

That, my friend, is a very dangerous place. It takes on a life of its own, inside you. You begin to define success by your dream. Reason becomes blurred. You can begin to reject wise counsel, constantly feeling like, they just don't understand.

I understand this. I've done it. And if I'm not very careful, open to correction and surround myself with strong people rather than "yes men," I can do it again. None of us are exempt. If you think for even a moment that you're exempt from this, you're kidding yourself. You've just taken the first step toward it. Anytime you think you're above anything, you're setting yourself up to go around that mountain just one more time.

You can never take ownership of what you allow God to do through you. Oh, I guess you can. And you can get away with it for a while, maybe even years. God is very patient. But sooner or later your motives will be revealed. There is nothing that will be hidden. And be assured, he will not share his glory with a man. The cost of you taking ownership of what God does through you is way too high.

And you will be tested in this. You will be tested as Joseph was, by family, sex and power. You will be tested in the areas of the lust of the eye, the lust of the flesh and the pride of life. You will be tested as to whether or not you can place your dream on the altar and sacrifice it, or be poured out like a drink offering, if he so desires. It's probably important for you to understand the drink offering as described in Scripture. Do a word search and study about it.

For everything God has for you, Satan has a counterfeit. Every counterfeit looks good. It will taste good, at least for a season.

And it will feel good, usually, for a while. Satan can come disguised as an angel of light. So pray for wisdom. Pray for discernment.

Don't be led by opportunity. I cannot count the number of times people have said something to me like, "This is so awesome, it must be God." "Only God could open this door." I used to say those kind of things and believe me, they are not always God. Opportunity will eat your lunch. Open doors do not always represent what God has for you. Be careful. Listen to God. Get counsel. Obey God.

Remember, lasting transformation in your heart comes from time with God. That's where the fruit of the Spirit is watered and begins to flourish in your life. Don't let busyness or business or opportunity or anything else come between you and time with God. The people that partner with God will cherish the times in their secret place with the Most High.

Don't be robbed of the joy of being where you are now, just because you're not where you will be. I think this is one of the most subtle thiefs that exist. Appreciate where you are now, who you're with and what you're doing. Honor all people. Enjoy the journey.

> The will of God for your life starts not with what you're doing, but in how you do what you're now doing.

Realize the will of God for your life does not begin when you get to another job, another company, another country, or another assignment. The will of God for your life starts not with what you're doing, but in how you do what you're doing right now. It starts in your heart.

When your heart is truly turned toward God and you begin to mature, your inner thoughts and conversations with others will be less and less about money, material wealth, "prosperity" and personal achievement, and more about what God is doing in your heart today, hearing the voice of God, insight and application of scripture.

One day my friend Don Hodges was praying and said, "God, I can't do this.... There are many other people more suited and better than me for this." He said God answered him with, "I know. That's exactly why I asked you. I can use people that know they can't do it."

It is an adventure.

The adventure you were born for—

Chapter 9

The Next Step to the Next Step— Accepting Responsibility and Becoming Accountable

The next step to your next step is something you can do that doesn't take any money, doesn't take anyone else to help you or agree with you, doesn't take much time, and yet is one of the foundational cornerstones for you reaching your destiny.

The next step to the next step is something that happens in your spirit. Down deep in the center core of your heart, you buy into the belief that there's more for you, that God does have a plan for your life, and you have the ability to go after it. You start buying into this, and things will start to happen to propel you into the most adventurous experience of your existence. You see...

Things are birthed in the spirit before they're birthed in the natural.

> The natural always has to give way to the Spirit of God.

I find that most people have trouble communicating to me what they really feel called to do. They may feel inadequate or fear that I'll laugh at them. I think most people have never even told another person what their hearts' desire is. Usually, they have only a general concept, not having spent any time at all on the details, even though they may have carried these beliefs in them for years and years.

I ask you, are you willing to accept responsibility:
- For your calling?
- For your gifts, skills and talents?
- For your dreams?
- For your errors?
- For your word?

- For your words?
- For your debts?
- For your time?

Will you now accept full responsibility for your past? If you say yes here, it means you're not pointing a finger of blame at anyone for anything in your past. This takes a lot of guts and maturity.

Will you now accept full responsibility for your present? If you say yes here, it means you're not pointing a finger of blame at anyone for anything in your life. This includes everything from who you are, where you are, where you've failed, what you've done, and what you haven't done.

Why do I ask this? Why is this absolutely necessary?

Because if you don't accept responsibility now for where you are, you won't be proactive in taking the next steps to mature and change your present circumstances and move closer to the partnership with God that's yours. It is yours, if and only if you go after it.

If you don't accept responsibility for where you are, you'll be sitting around waiting on God while he is patiently waiting on you. You'll be waiting on him for some big break or miracle and he's waiting on you to grow up, accept responsibility and go after what he's already provided for you.

> You can do what God has called you to do, but you can't do it man's ways.

You can change your circumstances. You do have choices. You have many choices before you.

My friend, Don Hodges, told a coworker the other day, "You're going to be sick all your life. You're never going to get well." The person was shocked and asked why. Don told them, "Because you're not doing anything differently to grow out of the situation you're in. And because of that, you'll always be in it."

That little story is applicable here to all of us. If we're blaming something or someone for our circumstances and what we have and where we are, we can never go forward.

If you will accept responsibility for your past and present, then you can do something about your future.

If you can do that, then I want to fuel your vision. I want to fuel your vision of what God can do through you if you let him.

I want to encourage you. You can do what God has called you to do. You can accomplish what God has called you to accomplish.

But you can't do it man's way.
- You can't do it the way of money.
- You can't do it the way of the world.
- You can't do it the way of "me first."

You can do what God has called you to do. But no flesh can glory in it. God will not share his glory with a man.

The eyes of God are going to and fro about the earth looking for men and women that will say, "Yes. Yes, God. I will give you all the glory."

If you want to be one of the people that will say to God, "Yes to your ways, yes I will let your wisdom and power flow through me," and you'll say "No, Lord, I won't take the gold or the glory, it is all yours," here's what I want you to do.

Begin to accept responsibility for your dream, for what God has called you to do.

Write it down. One of the most important steps in taking responsibility for your vision, your dream, your heart's desire is to write it down, in detail. Don't defer it, define it.

Whether it is typed or handwritten on a yellow pad makes no difference. The important thing is to begin. Write it.

Don't defer it. Define it. Write this as a document between you and God. Begin it now. Not next week or next month or next year. Now. No matter how far-fetched you feel it is from your present circumstances, do it and do it now.

Don't have a clue how to begin? Then write a letter to God. Keep it simple to start with. You can even use something like this:

Dear God,
     I don't know how to do all this, but here I am.
     I believe in you and I believe that you are a rewarder of those who diligently seek you. And I'm seeking you now.
     I may be puzzled about where I am in my present circumstances compared to what I feel you have told me, but I want your correction. I don't want to be a wayward child. Correct me where I'm wrong. Affirm me where I'm right. Direct my paths. Direct my emotions, my feelings, my responses, please.
     For some time now, I have had in my heart that you want me to be involved in (State here in simple language
                what's in your heart).

I acknowledge I cannot do this without you, and I don't want to do it without you. I have no idea how this can come about through me. But God, I'm willing to be used of you any way you want. Here I am God. Use me. Lead me step by step. Thank you.

Date it. Sign it.

If you want to share it with me, mail me a copy.

Tape it to your bathroom mirror or put it in some really conspicuous place.

This will begin the process of you taking responsibility for your dream more than anything else I know.

Now, this is not a document that you create and then put in some drawer only to be pulled out in a year.

> "Turn me away from wanting any other plan than yours. Revive my heart toward you"
> Psalms 119:37 TLB.

You are creating a living, dynamic document. This document will grow as you grow. This document will grow as your relationship with God grows and your godly character increases. This document will expand as you focus on it and God shares more revelation with you about it.

This is a document that you should read often, at least once a week. Read it and if no additions or modifications come to you about it, then just pray over it. Talk to God about it just like you would talk to me about it. As time goes on, you will receive additional insight about the parts of it that are right and the parts that need to be changed. Parts of it will expand and parts of it will shrink. You will modify it over and over as time goes on.

Are you really serious about this? Then start carrying a reduced-sized copy of the key points of it with you in your purse or shirt pocket or wallet, everywhere you go. If nothing else, this makes you more conscious of it. You'll think about it more and pray about it more.

I remember so well the day I was on the carpet in my home praying and I felt God tell me to get up and write the plan for GodinBusiness, and to write it in the normal business fashion. I thought I should be praying. Honestly, I wanted to pray. And actually, it was easier and more enjoyable to pray than it was to get up and go write that plan. But it became so intense in me that I knew, without a doubt, not to get up and begin that plan was to disobey. So I went upstairs, turned on the computer and began.

Then almost every day for weeks when I would start to pray, I felt God compel me, strongly, to get up and go write. Go write that plan. Go get on paper the vision of what was in my heart. And so I did. I resisted a few times briefly, but then I began to realize, this was a call to action.

I spent most of the next couple of weeks typing out the first "GodinBusiness" plan. It was fulfilling, but it wasn't fun and it definitely wasn't easy. Even though I could give some voice to what was inside me, getting it in writing forced me to crystallize in my mind what was important and what was not, what I felt was from God and what wasn't. The choice of words and sentences became all-important.

You see, getting all that on paper was another major, significant part of birthing what God has for me to do. That first plan comprised about forty pages. I had a section in it which listed many of the foundational premises from which I now write. It was a part of the birthing process.

If you omit the writing down of what's inside you, you circumvent part of the birthing process and you'll delay your maturing process. You'll be forever "verbally" bound and lack focus. While you may think you're being so successful, your emotions and circumstances will bounce you around and carry you on a ride that is far harder to steer and takes much longer and requires more emotional energy and money than a well planned, written, focused approach.

> It was fulfilling, but it wasn't fun. And it definitely wasn't easy.

A dream in writing is the beginning of a plan.

66

But a plan is almost worthless unless you voluntarily become accountable for it. I want you to become accountable to God for what he has placed in you. And the more accountable you become to God for your dream, the quicker he can help you mature and bring it into being.

I see people walking around everywhere that are incredibly talented but never work in the area of their passion or their dream. I don't want you to be one of them. That's one of the main reasons I'm writing this book. I want you to do your dream and I want you to partner with God to do it. You can do what God has for you to do.

> There is no growth without a sense of accountability and the acceptance of responsibility.

You can do...what you were born for....

"I cried out to him with my mouth; his praise was on my tongue. If I had cherished sin in my heart, the Lord would not have listened; but God has surely listened and heard my voice in prayer. Praise be to God, who has not rejected my prayer or withheld his love from me!" Psalms 66:17-20.

Chapter 10

If You're Going to Partner with God– You Have to Know His Voice

Sometimes:

- I hear words.
- I think thoughts.
- I have a knowing.
- I have a sense that…
- It just seems right.
- I have no clue.
- I blow it.
- I think he's silent.
- I think he doesn't care how I do it.
- I have a recurring thought.
- Often, he speaks through his Word.

Not long after I had started my own business, while still officing out of my home, a well-known businessman called and came by to talk with me about working with him on a large project he was planning. As we talked, I heard within me the word "ignominy." I couldn't remember what ignominy meant, but by the time he left, I felt more concern than I felt peace.

I found a dictionary and looked up the meaning of ignominy. It said, "reproach." It would have been very easy for me to override that caution and launch into that project. I was just starting my business, and I wanted to feel like this was a gift from God.

> The way I felt about this opportunity didn't seem to match up with the way I wanted to feel about it.

I wanted to say, "Oh, God, thank you for bringing me this big project and giving me the desires of my heart. What a wonderful opportunity God. *Only you* could have opened a door like this for me, causing me to get paid so well for this large project, working with these well-known people. Oh, God, you're awesome."

That's what I wanted to say and feel, but I kept thinking about "ignominy." I prayed about it for a couple of days and called the man and declined any involvement. The project went ahead without me but before it was over, it got complicated and messy. It got bogged down and ceased operation before completion. I don't think anyone got paid for all the work they did.

That one recurring word to me from the Holy Spirit, or should I say that counsel given to me by "my partner" during that conversation with a prospective client, saved me from many wasted hours and much grief.

It seems like "my partner" is a man of few words. There are so many ways he could have addressed me to let me know that the opportunity before me was not of him. If I was trying to caution my son or daughter to decline an offer I thought was wrong, I'd probably be trying to wave a big, red flag before them or shout the words, "Don't do this."

His way with me, that time, was to whisper one word a few times in my spirit. As I sought him about it over those next few days, I felt no peace. So that time I had a red flag in the form of a recurring word, ignominy, and a red flag of no peace.

As I seek God about options and decisions, I often have no direction whatsoever. Many times though, I tend to sense a sweet, deep peace that I feel like is his blessing on it.

Sometimes I have the opposite of peace, an unrest of sorts, a caution. How do I describe it? I think it's similar to me trying to tactfully let someone know that what they're thinking is not what I'm thinking.

It's sort of like someone asking me if I want to go to a restaurant that I don't care for. I may pause a couple of moments, maybe tilt my head a bit, and say without much enthusiasm, "Well, okay." It's kind of hard to put on paper, but there's just a slight reluctance somehow. My body language, my hesitation, my voice should be enough to communicate my true desires.

This unrest is kind of like a question mark inside of me. It's sometimes so big that it's like fireworks going off inside me. But most often, it's just a slight hesitation. It's something in me that wants to delay it or know more before I decide. Sometimes it is very slight. It may be different with you.

You may describe how God gives you a "check" in your spirit some other way, but somehow, he will communicate with you and warn you when things are not right, if you let him.

Always? No. Most of the time. Why not all the time? I don't know. He's God. I'm not.

Back when I was in college, I decided I wanted a Corvette. I didn't have much money but I began looking diligently for one. It didn't take me long to decide exactly what I wanted. I wanted a 327 engine, a T-top roof, and a 4-speed transmission. I did not want a hardtop or a convertible, and I didn't want the 427 engine. I looked at dozens of Corvettes over a period of several months. I found that most of them were run ragged. I could afford those. The ones that were really taken care of well were always too expensive for me. But I kept looking.

One night I knelt down by my bed with my hands raised to him and said, "Jesus, I love you," as I have done for probably twenty-five years, and I clearly heard him say to me, "Ted, tomorrow you'll get your Corvette." Oh, man! I knew that was the voice of the Lord to me. So I thought, what is my part? What else should I do? The only thing I could think of was to set my alarm early and read the newspaper first thing to check it for any available Corvettes. So I did.

> God said to me, "Ted, tomorrow you'll get your Corvette."

The next morning I got up early and read the paper. There were three Corvettes in it. But one had a 427 engine, one was a hardtop, and one was a convertible. I read those advertisements over and over and finally closed the paper and said to God something like, "I don't know how you're going to do this, but I still believe I heard your voice." I went back to bed.

A few hours later, Dad called me from Charleston (about a hundred miles away from where I was in school) and said, "If you're really determined to get a Corvette, I think you should come look at this one." I immediately got on my motorcycle (that's all I had at the time), drove to Charleston and went with Dad to look at it and bought it on the spot.

It was a gorgeous, one-owner, four-year-old, T-top Corvette with a 327 engine and 27,000 actual miles. It was immaculate, affordable and exactly what I wanted. I drove that car four years, 60,000 miles, and sold it for almost twice what I paid for it. Yep, God spoke to me that night about one of the desires of my heart, a Corvette.

Not long after I had begun my own business, I did quite a lot of work for a small business and they owed me quite a bit but hadn't paid me for a while. I really needed the money. But God was very gracious. One day while working at my desk, God spoke to me and told me to call the owner of the business and tell him, "I want the money, I want it all, and I want it now."

I was pretty surprised. My response was, "Me? Tell *this* man that?" I just sat there and pondered that which I felt was from God. I decided to sleep on it. A day or two later it hadn't left me so I phoned him and, as tactfully as I could, said, "Sir, I want the money, I want it all, and I want it now." I just waited for a response. My heart was pounding. He finally said that he had just received a large check in the mail that day and to come on by his office for a check. He paid me in full.

During the last seventeen years of being in my own business, over and over God has confirmed that he wants to be involved in business. I have tasted his love and graciousness in a myriad of business circumstances involving everything from resolving shareholder conflicts to settling IRS disputes.

But, what does God know about what I do—my business, my making a living? What does God know about growing a business, profit margins, financial statements, advertising, sales, technology, budgets, employees, knowledge capital, vendor agreements, pricing, product development, one to one marketing, computer systems, planning, manufacturing, customer relationship management, auditing, shareholders, ad infinitum?

I submit to you that possibly the most important aspect of our job as owner, CEO, CFO, manager, director, employee, consultant, or whatever we are, is that we don't stand in the way of God and letting him speak to us and give us the wisdom to do what he wants done. Can you buy into this?

What if God knows some things we don't know? Is this far-fetched? What if he'd share them with us? Is that possible?

What if the primary modus operandi of our business is not to display the successful implementation and execution of our own wisdom, but of God's wisdom?

Does he not tell us repeatedly in the book of Proverbs that Wisdom cries out in the streets to be heard? Are we listening, or does the segregation of the sacred and the secular rule our thinking to the point that we're not even open to hearing his voice regarding business?

After being in business a few years, I started doing a lot of work for a very profitable company. The owner was older and began to talk about selling it. I got the brilliant idea of buying it, even though it was no little operation. The more I thought about it the more excited I got about it.

One day a friend of mine was in my office and I mentioned to him that I was thinking about buying that business. When I had given him a few details, he said to me very precisely, "What are you going to do if he says no, and feels like you've breached your loyalty as counsel to him, and you lose him as a client?" I thought his question to me was ridiculous and didn't give it the time of day.

I had been given counsel by an astute businessman whom I respected, but I was already so intently moving into my dream of owning that company that I didn't want to hear him. I didn't want to think about this great opportunity not being right. I wanted it! I thought this man's counsel to me was really a far-fetched idea that couldn't happen.

But that's exactly what happened. I made an offer. The owner rejected it. I lost the account. It was disaster. I lost the most lucrative business client relationship I'd had up to that time.

Looking back, God spoke very clearly to me through my friend that day. If I had simply had the wisdom to value his counsel and seriously consider what he told me, and pray about it with an open heart, I am totally confident I would have heard Wisdom let me know not to proceed with that offer. I would have then saved myself and my client much hurt and grief, and I'd probably have had that client a long time. I may have actually been able to buy that company at a later date.

> I thought his counsel to me was ridiculous and didn't give it the time of day. But that's exactly what happened. I lost the account. It was disaster.

You see, I fell in love with the idea. God tried to speak wise counsel to me through a friend. I rejected it and the cost was high, much too high.

God cares about what concerns us. He cares about the details. He wants to be involved with the daily operations of our life in a way that allows him to show himself strong, and yet help us mature and develop our own faith and relationship with him.

What's important here is that God speaks today. Many people think he doesn't speak because they don't hear him. Some are disillusioned because they thought they heard God in their lives at some point, but the result was not like they had anticipated. It's so easy then to feel hurt, be disappointed, and allow your relationship with him to dwindle.

Remember, there are many voices in this world, and most of them are all too eager to speak their agenda and try to influence you for their purposes. Developing your discernment of the voice of God is a process. It takes time, but it is worth every bit of it. John 10:27 says, "My sheep listen to my voice; I know them, and they follow me." And Jeremiah 29:13 says, "You will seek me and find me when you will seek me with all your heart."

> What's important here is that God speaks today. And you can hear him.

To recognize the voice of the Master, you must spend time with him. The more time you spend in humility at his feet, the more you will learn his voice. The more you get to know him, the more you will experience him calling you to spend time with him.

It's not a one-way street. You won't always spend time together just at your convenience or desire. He also has the desire to spend time with you, and believe me, *he will let you know it*. It may not be anything for you like what I say here, but somehow, I want you to know to anticipate his tugging at your heart and encourage you to respond accordingly.

Years ago, even as a teenager and somewhat later, I would sometimes feel "down." Back then we called it being moody. I would feel like I wasn't in a good mood. After my prayer life got some life in it, I began to realize that this uneasy feeling was a call to pray. It was the Holy Spirit of God asking me to spend time with him. He wanted to hear from me and be with me.

For years now, as soon as I feel a caution, an uneasy feeling, or feel down or depressed at all, anxious or concerned, I know how to respond. I respond by getting alone with God and pouring myself out to him—my love, my worship, my trust, my requests, etc. Sometimes I find that the feeling that compelled me to pray will leave me after talking with God just a minute or two. Sometimes it is five, ten, twenty minutes or more. Sometimes it's an hour or more.

But I'm always surprised how often it's just a few minutes. I think it's similar to the way I so often want to talk with my wife, Barbi, for just a few minutes. I often go sit down in the room she's in and talk a few minutes, cover what was on my mind, and then go back to working or writing or whatever. Could it be that God tries to do the same with us?

I wouldn't be surprised if there are many people who feel God's tug and try whatever they can to get rid of it because they don't know what it is. They don't know what to do with it. They cover it up with pills, sports, entertainment, and anything they can get to get rid of it.

Sometimes I don't get "through," or "finished," or feel "complete," and that feeling does not leave me. Sometimes I try to ignore it or I have to go pick up the kids or have a pre-arranged appointment. Sometimes as I do other things, that feeling will leave pretty quickly. Sometimes it stays until I spend time with him again. And I never know which it will be. But this I know, over the years, year after year, time after time, that feeling is a call to the secret place, the place I talk and spend time with him alone. It's where he has all of my attention and I am focused on him alone.

Occasionally I feel that call to pray so intensely that I first check in with my family to make sure everyone is okay. I begin going down the list. Where's Barbi? Is she okay? I'll call her to make sure and ask about her, the kids and briefly let her know why I'm asking. I'll call and check in with my kids if they aren't with Barbi. I may even call Mom or my sister. Once I know they're all okay, I know I'm to pray for something and even though I don't know what it is for at the moment, I go to him.

I've learned that my prayer time is often for something future, sometimes later that day, sometimes months away. I've learned that anxiousness will at some point pass from me if I don't respond to it. But I know it is the call of God asking me to intervene, to pray, to pave the way for something, to pray protection for something or someone. I've had times that I began to pray, often out loud, focusing on the Most High and worshipping him, that I begin to know what I'm praying for. Sometimes I never know.

Sometimes I didn't pray and later found myself in a certain situation that, somehow in my spirit, I knew I was to have covered in prayer before it happened.

Sometimes I realize that I'm dealing with something or some situation that I have already prayed about in the past. When that happens, I'm always so thankful. God is so kind and so gracious. So many times he'll ask us to pray about things yet to come.

> Whether or not God was, or is, in something should not be determined by the presence of money, or by our society's definition of success.

So please understand that God is God and we are not. He has his own ways of coming to us and "asking" us to spend time with him. When those times come, and they will, we have a choice. Will we fill our schedule every minute? Or will his beckoning be something of importance that compels us to rearrange our schedule to take time with him?

I'd like to say that every time I feel that tug to pray that I receive it joyfully. I haven't. I'd like to say that whenever I feel some great concern in my soul, an anxiousness, that I welcome it and joyfully and quickly rearrange things to accommodate his leading. Sometimes, truthfully, I dread it because I have my day planned and I don't want to change it. But that's my fleshly response wanting to stay in control and I've learned that. Each time this happens, I choose. I realize that I should be interpreting this each time as him taking my hand, asking me to come to him. Think of it—the very God of heaven and earth will come and tug at our hearts to let us know that he wants *us* to commune with him. How very precious this is. Can you try to really grasp what I'm saying here?

It is so very important for you to comprehend this fact:

God will compel you to spend time with him.

God will come to you and compel you to spend time with him. Period. You will respond. Period. How you respond to these times will have a direct bearing on what you do the rest of your life and whether or not you really do fulfill your divine destiny in partnership with him. You have a choice. You are the one to decide what you want.

One of the most life-impacting statements ever made to me was when Pastor Joel Budd said, "You can have all of God you want." That was revelation to me. Up to that point in my life I had always felt that there was some station to which I was called and I hoped to reach it, somehow, whatever it was.

Somehow implicit in this revelation about having all of God I wanted was the realization that my own choices, my own desires, discipline and diligence in pursuing God are not limited. The more I seek him the more I find him. The closer I draw to him the closer he draws to me. The more I share my life with him the more he shares his life with me.

The result? More relationship, less religion, rules and duty. Relationship. I get to know him. And when I'm in his presence, my humanness and character are changed and forged more and more into the likeness of Christ. What a privilege to talk with our Creator. I have that privilege. You have that privilege. Are you exercising your privilege?

This is an adventure, a journey that takes us from the bondage of religious works and rules, money, dependent relationships and immaturity to one of freedom and maturity. This journey is for life. This is the abundant life.

The rest of our lives will be spent in getting to know him, not just about him, and understanding what it means to partner with the Holy Spirit of God. We'll begin to understand his ways more and have the character of the living, speaking Christ formed in us, so that when he breathes on us and we begin to experience the true synergy of his partnership, and supernatural achievements take place through us, we don't topple ourselves over, stumbling on our own pride thinking "we did it."

We all, at times, have looked for signs, miracles, and prosperity. God is looking for those who will sit at his feet so that he can impart himself into them. Those who play games with God will forever be immature, never fully enjoying their adventure and never achieving the realization of their dream, their potential destiny.

> Man looks for success. God is looking for those that success won't corrupt. Will you be one?

One of the problems with our immaturity is that when God speaks to us and we interpret that into action, we then think it's complete, not realizing that it is always one part of a larger process. And, God is into process.

Remember, God worked one day. He sat back and looked at it. He evaluated it and said, "This is good."

The next day, he worked on it again. He built upon what he had done the previous day. He added to it. He fashioned more and more of his creativity upon the earth. And at the end of the day, he sat back and looked at it. He evaluated it again and said, "This is good."

The next day, he worked on it again until he felt it was complete. It took time. It was a process. It was not a quick work. He kept examining and evaluating his own handiwork and where he was in the process and kept working at it until it was complete.

How often do we get a word or direction from God and feel like, "this is it," and off we go to camp in that one revelation, that one area of wisdom, parking there and spending our life in it, instead of sitting back, looking at it, evaluating it, and saying, "This is good, but it is not complete yet. There's more." How often do we then go ahead and keep working on it the second day?

I want you to do what you were born for—whatever it is—find the cure for cancer, heart disease, for business failures far exceeding business successes, discover technologies yet undreamed. Help women become as accepted in the marketplace as much as men and in any endeavor they choose. Maybe you are one to bring more creativity and healing into this generation and for generations to come.

Get quiet before God and learn to know his voice, and he'll speak to you about what's on his mind for you....

Chapter 11

What's the Deal with Gifts, Skills, Abilities and Talents?

Many Christians seem to have a significant, ongoing problem in their lives dealing with the balance between what they do and what God does. Maybe we all have that problem, but if so, I think too many Christians have bought into the belief that since they love God and read the Bible and pray, they don't have to work as hard to achieve excellence as does a person who has no concept of partnership with God.

I think that many Christians have a problem even knowing what excellence really is. Many seem to get to a point that they think will get them by, and then cast out some little prayer to get them and their situation "blessed."

> We Christians are often wimps—using our Christianity as a facade for our laziness and less than excellent work.

Many Christians simply do not have the work ethic that compels them to be diligent enough to compete in the real world. This is tragic. I think this problem is epidemic.

If we're going to accomplish anything, we have to *work* to develop the gifts he's given us. And if you don't buy into this you're deceived.

We all have respect for those who work diligently at developing what God has given them. No matter what God has given you, you must develop it. You must be disciplined and focused. And you pay a price to do that.

There's no question in my mind that there are many people walking all around us who have the potential of Edison, Carver and Einstein but they will never amount to a hill of beans because of their lack of vision, focus and discipline.

You might say many don't have the opportunity to develop their gifts and skills because of their socio-economic status, or because of some other reason. That might be true to some extent, but *I submit to you that no matter where you are, what you have or don't have, if you start diligently pursuing God with a humble heart, God will somehow get to you what you need to accomplish his purposes in your life.*

If you want to partner with God, if you want him to anoint you and your efforts, please buy into the importance of being the best that you can be, right now, at whatever you are and whatever you do, with whatever you have. God does not anoint laziness.

Why my emphasis here on excellence when I started off addressing gifts, skills, abilities and talents? Because excellence is important to God.

Many of us have skills, abilities and talents. We may even be really gifted in some areas. But I think too often, we come to God expecting him to catapult us into another realm of "success" just because we know he can. We don't really want to pay the price for excellence. Our innate human nature wants the easy route. We want a miracle. Too often, we come to God thinking he'll do most of the work for us.

> Note that the people God gave "special skill" here were already known as "experts," and "craftsmen."

Who in the world was Bezalel and why should you know about him? When God gave the instructions about the building of the Temple, not only did he give many specific instructions about the blueprints to be followed, he also anointed the workers to build it. You can read about it Exodus 31.

"The Lord also said to Moses, 'See, I have appointed Bezalel…and have filled him with the Spirit of God, giving him great wisdom, ability, and skill in constructing the Tabernacle and everything it contains. *He is highly capable* as an artistic designer of objects made of gold, silver, and bronze. *He is skilled*, too, as a jeweler and in carving wood. And I have appointed Oholiab...to be his assistant; moreover, *I have given special skill to all who are known as experts,* so that they can make all the things I have instructed you to make..." (Exodus 31:1-6 TLB), emphasis mine.

Notice several things: Bezalel was anointed by God who "filled him with the Spirit of God," to do what? Preach? Witness? Do "ministry?" No. He was anointed by God for his regular job of, what? What was that? Construction!

And what else is significant here? God didn't just anoint some nice people to go build this special place. He anointed the experts. They had already learned, applied themselves diligently, and did their work with excellence. They were known as skilled workers. They weren't mediocre, barely-get-by workers. They had a work ethic that compelled them to excellence before they were ever "employed" and "anointed" to build the temple. *They were ready* to be used by him.

How many people are waiting on God to use them, but they are not yet ready to be used by him? They haven't learned, applied themselves diligently, and worked toward excellence. They haven't studied and continued to refine their skills. They sit back and say they're still waiting on God.

I want you to be in the category of people that work diligently to refine, enhance and broaden their skills so that when God opens doors for you, your skills will be as mature as your Godly character.

Skill you can replicate, like riding a bicycle or playing tennis. You can do it anytime you want to. You may have been born with what seems to be a talent in a particular area, but you have to work at refining that talent until it becomes useful to you and to others. Skills have to be developed over time, with discipline and diligence.

There is no mastery of skill without discipline. No matter how gifted you are, you must master your skill. We must discipline ourselves more to accomplish and achieve breakthroughs in areas such as the arts and sciences, as well as business.

God has taught me many things about him through my family.

For instance, my daughter, Amy, plays the piano. She's good. She's really, unbelievably, incredibly good. And she's still a teenager. She has played in many piano competitions and won numerous trophies, ribbons and awards for her playing.

Everywhere she plays, people young and old come up to me and say things like: "Oh, Amy is so gifted." "Amy is so anointed." "I'd give anything to play like that."

Amy's accomplishments already are many, but I often wonder if any of the people that mention her "gifting" have any idea of the thousands of hours she has spent practicing piano—*thousands and thousands of hours*. Since she was knee high to a duck, she has played the piano and loved it. During times when we as a family were doing yard work or painting or whatever, if Amy wanted to practice, we let her. We rarely, if ever, pulled her off the piano to do other things.

> Yep, Amy is gifted. She's awesome. She's anointed. That's right. But she's paid a price for the excellence she's attained that few realize.

When she was about ten years old, she was on the piano bench one day talking with me and said with such deliberateness and determination, "Daddy, I've decided I'm going to be good on piano." And she is. She plays classical, jazz, worship and composes songs from heaven. She's an angel and I assure you I'm not prejudiced at all!

The point here is this. People listen to Amy play now and it's easy for them to say she's gifted and anointed. But she has been diligent. She has disciplined herself. She has practiced many hours that I know she would liked to have been doing other things—playing, talking with friends or just goofing off.

I know the number of times she's practiced until her arms hurt and she would come to me, asking me to pray for her because they hurt so much. I know the number of times she's come to me, to my son, and my wife, asking us to rub her neck because it was aching. I've seen her shake her arms during practice times when I knew her arms were hurting. Yet she would continue to practice and play for hours.

She has been focused on her goal and she's paid a price. And most people never see that or think about it. Most people don't think about the price they have to pay for excellence.

Don't compare yourself to Amy. Don't compare yourself to me or anyone else. Go to God, over and over, and present yourself as a living sacrifice to be used by him, for him. Commune with him, and then get up and pursue excellence whether you're a student, banker, baker or candlestick maker. If you can do better, do it.

> We must mature in these areas. We must choose to grow up.

Although skill can be replicated at will, anointing is not the same way. Anointing is not something you can replicate any time you want it. You can't turn it on and off at will. Anointing is not simple to define. Anointing comes from God. It may be momentary, as it often is, and it may be semi-permanent. Anointing can be inside you, internally, and it can be up on you and be very visible. I don't think we have much wisdom when it comes to dealing with the anointing, especially when we're talking about it in the daily operation of making a living.

The anointing of God comes to us for many different tasks. In my work, I don't need the anointing to outrun a chariot (1 Kings

85

18:46), or make an ax head float (2 Kings 6:5-6). I need the anointing of God to understand the direction a company should go to grow. I need the anointing of God to understand how a company should be structured, how to help its leadership focus on what's important, how to get the management team in agreement and working together, how to implement strategic plans and tap into all the knowledge capital they have.

So how does God help me do this? In my work as a consultant to various companies, sometimes in meetings, I will know that God is speaking to me inside. I may suddenly realize the people and forces behind certain circumstances and know what to do. Sometimes I'll be at my desk or computer and be asking God for discernment and wisdom. Sometimes I'll be on the floor of my office with a company's organization chart, financial statements, and strategic plan papers spread everywhere, praying over them and asking God what to do.

Sometimes direction seems like it's so very divine, precious and exciting. Sometimes it seems easy. But more often than not, it's hard, complex and time consuming work. I operate with all of my skill and ability, drawing on all the experience I have, while at the same time, calling out to God for help and direction.

> I'm convinced he's more interested in us maturing than we are, so that he can do what he wants done in the earth.

It's not just God doing things through me. I'm not a robot. And it's not just me producing what I can do only with my natural skills and abilities. It's a cooperative, joint effort.

Somehow I believe that's right. Look at the relationship I have with my kids. I want to be at their side and help them and let them feel my love and support. But I also want them to grow up and mature, develop their own discernment and good judgment, use and value all that I've imparted into them, and fulfill their own destiny. But I don't want them leaving me out of their lives while they're doing all that. There's always this dynamic balance between what I do for them and what they must do themselves to grow and mature.

I still want to be "of counsel" to them. I still want them to feel my love, support and encouragement that they can, in fact, do what they believe God has placed within their hearts to do, but I can't do it for them. There are times that, in order for their faith and character to grow, they must apply all that they've learned, all I've imparted into them, all of their own discernment and diligence, mix it up with their own faith and prayer, and go take action.

Wisdom, I think, is the intersection of truth, knowledge, understanding, timing and balance. It is a course of action to be wise so that there is gain, increase, advancement, and maturity rather than loss, decrease, demotion and immaturity.

I'm sure I've struggled with the concept of excellence many times since I started my own consulting business almost twenty years ago. Excellence is a moving target. What excellence was yesterday is not necessarily considered excellence today. Our culture, community and expectations of service continue to be redefined. Excellence is an ongoing quest for everyone who wants to do all that God has for them.

God is a living, speaking God. Spend time with him alone, make it a priority, study and value his Word, value and record his words to you, remove any barriers between you and him.

As you spend time with him he will direct your path. He will lead you to information and tools he wants you to have. He will cause divine appointments and connections. He will make himself known to you. He will reveal himself and his character to you from his Word and by his voice. He will give you instructions. And he wants them carried out with excellence, with diligence, with effort, which means, you have to work at it.

You will pay a price to partner with the living God. It begins with simply deciding what you want. Do you want to *know*

God? Do you want to know him enough to spend time with him and get to know his voice and his Word? Do you want to know his values and what's important to him? What does he consider excellence?

Are you willing to ask him, to seek him diligently about it?

The more your character conforms to the image of the living, speaking Christ, the more he can come to you and upon you, anointing you to do, to know and to achieve things beyond your wildest dreams.

I am sounding a wake-up call for you to go to God more and more about the details of your work. Can you buy into the belief that he wants to be involved? Ask him to be involved. Go to him often, many times a day. Partner with him and he'll partner with you. Seek God. Seek excellence.

Ask him to anoint all the tools of your trade, anoint you to understand and utilize financial statements, written plans, computers, microscopes, etc. Involve him in all that you do. Seek him with all of your heart. And you know what?

"I will be found of you, says the LORD" Jeremiah 29:14.

We all would like the anointing of God to help us achieve and accomplish great things, but I have to address these foundational, core concepts of excellence so that when we come to him and present him all that we are, he has something of excellence to work with.

Randy Hurst says that God doesn't need much from us, but he wants something. Even if the need is to feed 5,000 people and you only have a few fish to offer, you must give God something to work with, to mold, to fashion, to multiply.

Will you give him all of you, to work with, to mold, to fashion and let him multiply you... to do what he had you born to do?

Chapter 12

Communication

One of the most erroneous assumptions on our planet is that because we can talk, we can effectively communicate letting other people know what we mean and how we feel.

I suspect communication became tough after Adam and Eve ate of the forbidden fruit in the Garden of Eden. It must be a result of the fall of man (Genesis 3). And after the Tower of Babel incident where God scrambled their language, communication became even more difficult (Genesis 11:1-9). I'm not sure it's ever recovered.

Poor communication skills have cost us untold grief and pain, millions of broken marriages and millions of failed businesses.

If we could truly grasp the power of words, especially the spoken word, it would change us forever. The words we speak have a profound effect on us as we speak them, as well as on those who hear them. There is a burst of energy in every word that affects us both in the natural realm and in the spiritual realm.

> For you to achieve your dream, your divine destiny, you will probably need to increase your understanding of the fundamental aspects of communication.

We all need other people. None of us are called to work alone. We are called to work with other people. Because we interact with others, the ability to work synergistically depends tremendously on our ability to communicate effectively.

My teenage son, Christopher, and I go out for coffee together almost every night. Sometimes we talk at the coffee shop ten or fifteen minutes, but often we spend thirty minutes to an hour together there just talking. One night after spending over an hour there together in such great conversation, I asked him why he felt we had such great times together.

He said, "Well Dad, I think it's because we have such a profound respect for each other." Pretty neat coming from my then sixteen year old son. I loved it. What a compliment to both of us. What a compliment to my own Dad, Frank Cottingham, who took me out to coffee with him at least two or three times a week for years and years. We'd just talk—sharing our lives together. Those were precious, precious times together.

Actually, I'm not sure there's any true, personal communication without respect.

Communication among family members, coworkers and colleagues is so much more synergistic when it's not only an exchange of words but what I'll term "commune-ication." To commune means to converse intimately. That's more than just talking. It embodies your heart and motive and *how* you come together—what your attitude is and what you really want. You come together as equals to dialogue without a preconceived agenda of what you're trying to get out of the other person, or what you want to come out your way. There's a simplicity of sharing thoughts and ideas.

> Our communication is a reflection of our heart.

Communication when you want things to come out your way is not communication, it's negotiation. Okay, negotiation is communication, but it always has an agenda. Commune-ication occurs when you come together to commune. You may have a list of things you want to discuss, but you're not trying to control the outcome for your own best interest. True communing is never self-serving.

The deep, innate need we have for commune-ication is frequently thwarted by our lack of ability to communicate.

Maturity in communications allows us to disagree without any hint of trying to convince another person that we're right. Don't ever seek to justify yourself to be right in another person's eyes. Self-justification almost always ends with misunderstanding. Seek truth. Dialogue, share, ask questions. Don't make so many assumptions. Know that we're just not going to agree on everything, and that it's okay.

One of the most destructive forces among Christians has been our lack of maturity in communications, always thinking we're right and not allowing others to disagree with us and still remain

> We need to learn how to agree to disagree and yet keep our relationships in tact.

friends. We need to learn how to agree to disagree and yet keep our relationships in tact.

My Mom used to tell me so often growing up, "Theodore, be a gleaner." She told me that years before I even had an inkling as to what she meant. It is wise counsel for both you and me. When it comes to communication, we must learn how to eat the fish and spit out the bones. Be a gleaner. Take the good and leave the rest.

Listen more and have the other person's best interest in your heart. How many times are we thinking so intently about what we're going to say next that, even though we're smiling and nodding our heads, we're not really listening to the other person. We just don't care that much. We are much too quick to connect a couple of points and think we know what the other person means. We have not been taught the skill of listening. We need to learn.

As you spend time with the Father, your wisdom, understanding and knowledge of communication will increase. Things important to him will become important to you, and things unimportant to him will become unimportant to you. Your adventure will become more and more exciting. You will, undoubtedly, begin to notice a change in your communication with others. It may be ever so slight at first, but it will come. Getting closer to God causes your heart to change. As your heart changes your communication will change.

I suspect you'll begin to listen more and ask more questions. You'll respect people more. You might not be quite as quick to reply, pondering things more, valuing more the wisdom of others than in the past.

> There is no accountability without communication.

As you spend time with the Father, let the Holy Spirit teach you about all these things. Start studying the scriptures about communication. As you study, read, listen, pray and ponder, ask the Holy Spirit about these things. Say, "Holy Spirit, will you please help me understand communication?" And in due course, he will. I'm convinced, he'll always give us all we can handle, if we abide in him.

He will teach you how to talk if you ask him. And he'll teach you how to listen if you will let him. Transformation always takes place in his presence. If you ask according to his will, you will get it.

And believe me, it's his will that we take a massive step up in our ability to communicate with one another.

Learn to communicate. Learn to commune-icate.

Whatever dominates your communication will dominate your life. Whatever dominates your input will control your life.

What comes out of your life is a direct result of what you allow to be put into it.

Be a little more selective.

Chapter 13

Counsel, or
Have a Piece of Pie, Will You?

I heard a preacher years ago say, "When I order a piece of pie, I want it brought to me, placed before me, and I want to eat it at my pace. I want to eat as much of it or as little of it as I desire. I don't want it brought to me and smashed in my face." I didn't think much of it at the time.

However, one day a couple of years ago that little story came back to me in a flash along with a revelation: that's exactly how counsel should be given. You see, when I seek counsel from someone, I want to know what they think. I want them to put that counsel, as it were, before me on a plate so that I can choose all of it or a part of it. I want to be able to even disregard all of it without fear of hurting the one giving it, or having it affect our relationship in any way.

I want us to get a vision for what counsel is and isn't, how to give it and how to receive it. Counsel is information, advice, opinion, and recommendation. Counsel may be the result of research, investigation or experience. Counsel is guidance, direction, warning or suggestion. Counsel is usually what someone else believes.

Last night as I was discussing something with my teenage son, Christopher, he mentioned his thoughts about a given situation. When he finished, he asked me what I thought and I told him I felt the opposite way. Since we so often agree on things, he just looked at me waiting to see what I'd say next.

I then reached over and put my hand on him tenderly and said, "Son, it's okay to disagree with me. It's fine." He smiled so big. This was no life or death situation. We were merely discussing our opinions about something.

Counsel is not control. Counsel is not debate. Counsel is not trying to convince someone else we're right. Counsel is not trying to predetermine the outcome. Counsel liberates. Control restricts.

When my kids come to me now and ask about things, are they seeking my control? No, they're seeking my counsel. They want to know about my experiences and feelings. They want to ask questions and dialogue about real life situations. As teenagers now, they want to receive input and arrive at decisions on their own. They're maturing and developing into men and women, not just physically but in areas of responsibility, accountability and character.

> For you to reach your divine destiny, you need to understand counsel.

Counsel is brought and offered on a plate so that the leader, friend, colleague, spouse, parent or teen can consider it as they desire.

For you to reach your dream, you need to understand how to give counsel and how to receive counsel. As you seek wisdom, knowledge and understanding from others, you need to be wise and discern when people are giving you counsel and when they are merely trying to get you to do what they want you to do.

And, conversely, when others come to you for wisdom, knowledge and understanding, you should strive to give it to them without trying to get them to do what you think is best.

Learn to ask good, quality, sincere questions of those whose counsel you value. Learn to seek counsel. Learn to accept counsel. Be open to it. So many people are so wise in their own eyes that they seek no counsel from others and then they wonder why things don't work out for them. We all need other people.

Proverbs 20:5, KJV, says, "Counsel in the heart of man is like deep water; but a man of understanding will draw it out."

I've had the privilege of talking with some very wise and godly men, men that make me think, men that truly seek God and excellence at the same time. But you know what I've noticed about them? None of them talk much about what they do, what they know, what they've been through, what they've learned, what they've accomplished, or the revelation they've been given.

Almost invariably, these people that I so respect share their wisdom only when asked. I had to learn how to draw out the wisdom they have inside them—wisdom they really love to share—but don't, until they're asked.

If you're going to fulfill your dream and achieve what is in your heart, you cannot do it alone. God lets peoples' paths cross for a purpose. We have often forfeited the opportunity to learn a lot of wisdom, knowledge and understanding from others, because we haven't been men of understanding that draw it out of others.

As I ponder principles, situations, thoughts, scriptures, etc., I often mention them to my kids and ask them what they think. Sometimes they have not a clue. Other times they astound me with the wisdom that comes out of them. Many times I am aware that God is speaking directly to me through them. They often speak with such wisdom it makes me grab my pen and tablet to write down what they say. When revelation comes, I want it on paper.

Without wise counsel, destinies can be delayed, diverted and destroyed. Be wise and discern the hearts and motives of those you listen to. Their counsel can be as destructive as it can be constructive. They can build you up, help you leap-frog over known pitfalls, bring you their wisdom from God, and help catapult you into the realm of God's innovation and creativity. They can also do the opposite, even in the same meeting.

Isn't that what happened with Peter in Matthew 16:15-16? Jesus asked the disciples "Who do you say I am?" Peter answered, "You are the Christ, the Son of the living God." Then Jesus answered that Peter was blessed for this insight and that he would build his church upon that revelation.

Then in the next couple of verses, Matthew 16:22-23, we see Peter taking Jesus aside to "rebuke him." Jesus then spoke to Peter, "Get behind me, Satan! You are a stumbling block to me; you do not have in mind the things of God, but the things of men."

You see, one moment Peter was speaking divine revelation. And just a little bit later, Jesus said Peter was speaking things of men and not of God. Be wise. Pray for discernment.

We must remember this example and be wise as serpents and harmless as doves. We must learn to discern. Eat the fish, spit out the bones.

Counsel is a necessary ingredient in your adventure. Learn to seek it. Learn to be wise in drawing it out of those around you.

But don't swallow everything set before you.

Chapter 14

Control

Control is something that happens in our spirits when we decide we want another person to conform to the image we have for them so that they will serve our purposes.

We want others to be a certain way or do certain things. That behavior we seek from them may bring us money, prestige or status. But in every case, it is self-serving.

The subject of control is of crucial importance to your partnership with God because it greatly hinders the fulfillment of the destinies of both the one controlling and the one being controlled.

Control is rampant in church, in business and in families. Control is so common that we usually fail to recognize it, even when it's all around us in neon lights.

> Control is something that happens in our spirit when we decide we want another person to conform to the image we have for them.

Control is the invisible fence that holds us in the prisons of religion, relationship and money. It is the elevation of rules, rituals, performance and that which is temporal and false, above that which is everlasting and brings truth and freedom.

The concept of control is complex. That means it cannot be dealt with easily or lightly, and especially in such brief terms as in this one chapter. I still address it herein because I have felt so compelled by the Lord to do so.

Control is insidious, treacherous, seductive and yet often subtle. Its tentacles reach from the lowest income families and smallest businesses to the richest and most powerful families, businesses, governments, empires and ministries in the world. It knows no boundaries and runs roughshod over all of those without a revelation of the truth and freedom found in Jesus Christ.

Control emasculates a person. "Emasculate" means to castrate, to take away a person's ability to function fully and reproduce themselves.

When you take away from a person the ability to reproduce themselves—reproduce their gifts, skills, abilities, and talents in others—you create a void in that person that they *will* fill with something.

> Environments that should be free, but are highly controlled, foster depression, dependence and immaturity.

When a person cannot share who they are and what they have with others, the natural flow of their spirit gets stopped-up, causing confusion, hurt, disorder and discouragement.

The "stopped-up" person will "throw" themselves into anything they think will ease their soul and relieve some of their pain and disappointment. The "stopped-up" person often turns to, and immerses themselves in alcohol, sex, entertainment, cults, work, food, sports or religion. I think addictions are more a result of hurt and disappointment from being "stopped-up" than from any other reason.

We were born to reproduce ourselves.

God is into process and the maturing of his family. We should be also. The more we help people to truly *know* God for themselves, the more they will experience true freedom and maturity in their partnership with God—utilizing all of their gifts, skills, abilities and talents—not only to make a living, but to reproduce themselves in others.

The result? Excitement, enthusiasm and growth will take place in the body of Christ, with synergistic, exponential results in our families, businesses and churches. This, I believe, is the foundation of the revival that so many prophesy will come.

Why do we want to control other people so much? Maybe it's because of our own insecurities. Maybe we fear having people around us that know more than we do, that have more education than we do, or that we think are more qualified than we are. We might fear being exposed for what we really are. We might lose face in front of another person.

We fear this because our root identity is not in Christ. It's in what we do, our title, our position, our status, and how we think other people "perceive" us. Our insecurities and inadequacies drive us to be protective and do many things that make us stump our own toe and pierce ourselves through with many sorrows.

Every one of our lives produce fruit. Each of us produces the fruit of the Spirit or the fruit of control. Often we deal with people that seem to have the former until we question them, or challenge their assumptions, or even just try to dialogue with them intelligently. Then watch out, because that's when what is really on the throne of their heart usually comes out.

I've had people tell me about being in a wonderful church with a wonderful pastor until they communicated to the pastor that they felt they were to attend church elsewhere. The pastor then turned on them and began to make fun of them, telling them they had no ability to hear God. He did everything possible to convince them that if they wanted to stay in God's will for their lives, they had to stay right there in that church under him.

> Where arrogance abounds, control is close by.

That's called…control.

Go where you can grow, not just where you can serve.

There are those who will tell you to humble yourself where you are so that God can exalt you later, "in due season," referencing Galatians 6:9 KJV.

Now, if you humble yourself and submit where you are and you're in the wrong place, then you are not going to be exalted later. You're going to be disappointed and get hurt. It's just a matter of time. It may be months or it may be years. But you will eventually have a crushed spirit and no passion. Hope deferred will make your heart sick, as stated in Proverbs 13:12. Depression will set in.

If you're in the right place—the place of obedience to God rather than man—and seek God first, with all of your heart, mind, body and soul, you will, in due season, be exalted, promoted, and moved to the next step.

So the key? You have to be led by the Holy Spirit of God to discern for yourself whether or not you're in the right spot, the right church, the right job. Only you can answer that. No one else can answer that for you. It is one thing for God to tell you to humble yourself and wait. It's quite another for a man to tell you that. Seek and evaluate the counsel of man but obey only God.

> Obedience to God is better than sacrifice.

Now I want you to learn from me and from others, but I don't want you to be dependent upon me, or any other man, for what you should be getting from God yourself, directly. Let the Holy Spirit teach you and don't be dependent on any man, woman or institution.

There are people who control others, and there are those who are under the control of others. I don't want you to be in either category.

That which does not foster freedom and maturity fosters control and dependence. Control always has an agenda that is self-serving to the controller.

There are those who want to control everything. They want to make all the decisions and have everyone get permission from them for almost everything. They don't need anyone's help in knowing what to do, and they want no one's input. Nothing significant happens without their decision to do it. They'll control spouses, kids, bosses, colleagues, pastors, boards; everything they touch will have their imprint on it.

Then there are those who say they control nothing. They often have an attitude of, "Oh pity me. I'm a victim. I couldn't change anything if I tried. I have no choices in the matter. No one will listen to me or care so I'm not going to do anything." But often they control by refusing to advance.

Picture it. A man is leading a donkey when suddenly, the donkey sits down and then won't move. Tell me, who's in control, the man that was leading or the donkey that was following? I submit to you that at that point, the donkey is in control. Isn't that ironic that a follower can control? Suddenly, the leader becomes subject to the follower.

This can take place in your marriage, your job, wherever you are. If you've got key people in your life and organization who won't listen, learn, grow and advance with you, they can control a lot of territory by their "sitting down."

I think most people are either under the control of another person, or they control other people, or both. And the cost of this kind of thing? Oh. It's way too high.

The spirit of control may slip in disguised as an angel of light. Well-intentioned Christians who love and serve the Lord often move steadily along a path where they start doing what they want to do more than what God wants them to do. They begin to feel like it's more and more dependent on them to do whatever it is they're doing, "for God." Their "doing" gradually becomes more important to them than God. Perpetuating themselves, their status, their income, all become all consuming.

Ever so gradually, the god of "I want" and the god of control push Christ and humility off the throne of their heart. But take note here; that kind of person still has all the trappings, outward appearances and conversational terminology of true Christians, although Christ is no longer on the throne of their heart.

That's what deception is. Those people don't even realize that they've exchanged the Christ for the god of control. It can be businesspeople, parents, preachers, deacons, leaders, people just like you and me...deceived.

> Whatever you want to flourish, water it with freedom.

Control is very deceptive because not only do most people not realize they're controlling, but if approached or asked about it in any way at all, the controller will probably answer one of two ways. One is to be defensive and resent you insinuating that they are controlling. The other is more subtle but usually contains something about "doing what's best" for those they're controlling.

Millions of people are being robbed of pursuing their dream and their God-given destiny because they are being controlled by other people, or they won't give up their control of other people. Both are injurious and hinder their partnership with God.

Control in business has been epidemic. "Do as I say and don't ask questions." This message has been sent for years. "I don't care what all you can do for us, shut up and do your job. You've got a job description, go do it."

We tend to peg people, put them in a box and never let them out. We never think about all the ways our own people can help us because, traditionally, we just want them to do their "job."

It is no longer uncommon to find a person in one job that has more skill and talent in a completely different department. But there's seldom any openness of management to allow their people to operate in areas beyond what they've always done there.

How limiting. How sad. Why lose good people to another company where they'll be doing what you could have benefited from? Why don't you value them enough to give them the time of day and a forum to hear what they care about?

How often are we walking all over the gifts in the people who are there to help us? Why do we let them give us only what we think we want from them at that moment?

The box we draw around people could be likened to us always treating our children as little kids and never as our friends. We cast them into a position and never let them spread their wings and develop into full maturity. The cost of this? Oh, it's much too high.

More and more people have a bigger, better knowledge base, a wider range of skills and numerous talents that they're developing continually, and they want to use them. They *will* go where they can use them. If they can't find a place where they are valued and allowed to mature and spread their wings, they'll start their own business.

> In business we are better at controlling people and thwarting their creativity than releasing it.

And there are others that will forfeit their destiny for the sake of what they perceive as security, becoming miserable and resigning themselves to "victim-itus." These are the ones that become cynical and turn inward, blaming God, blaming the system, blaming everyone but themselves. We all have a choice. We all have many choices.

The businesses that flourish in the future will be the ones that recognize that their workers come to them with a multiple array of skill sets, and give them the opportunity to utilize them.

The businesses that flourish in the future will focus not on controlling their people, but on the opposite. They will provide multiple venues to free the creativity of each worker to allow all the gifts and wisdom within them to be used for their advancement and the advancement of the company. In every business are the seeds of additional streams of revenues if identified and developed.

Do what you've always done and you'll get less and less.

I've inflicted a lot of pain on myself and my family because of my ignorance, because of selfishness and because of my desire to control. I always did what I thought was right. But just because I did the best I knew how and did what I thought was right, did not make it right. Isn't a man always justified in his own eyes?

Since I began to receive revelation in this area, I no longer try to get my wife, Barbi, to be anyone other than who she is. I no longer try to get her to do anything that is not in her heart. I no longer attempt to conform her to any image other than what she is. And why would I? She's a wonderful, beautiful and bright woman and she loves God. If she wants to do something, I'm glad when she talks it over with me beforehand. I let her know my thoughts, feelings and preferences. I give counsel, but she makes her own decisions.

If she honors me or considers what I desire, it's her decision. I no longer try to make that happen. I take no steps to control what she does or does not do for me. Whatever she does with me or for me will be out of her own heart. I want her to be herself and mature and do all that's within her heart.

For example, Barbi surprised me the other day, mentioning that she's thinking about going back to school to get her masters degree in music. I said, "Great, I'm proud of you. Go for it." If that's growing in her heart, I want her to follow what she believes is right for her.

She surprised me again when she started writing articles that will become a book at some point. When she brought me those first rough drafts to read and tell her what I thought, I really encouraged her to pursue writing. I want her to use to the fullest every gift, skill, ability and talent she has. She's already put some of her short stories on her own Website. You can check them out at www.Barbi.org.

I want her to be herself. I don't want her to try to operate out of my expectations. Several years ago I addressed some of these issues in detail with her. I began to realize that she felt like she had to be a certain way and do certain things. I responded with what I could to try to free her from those feelings and to put no expectations on her at all, which I found, actually, was hard to do. But I worked on it, and I still work on it. When I put no expectations on her, and she puts none on me, we operate in so much more joy, freedom and laughter. It really is another whole level.

What are you doing to help your spouse flourish into the man or woman God has called them to be? Are you holding them back? Are you still trying to make them conform to an image you have for them? What about your kids?

What about your employees, your coworkers, even your boss? Are you empowering them to be all they can be? Are you free of the control of man and religion?

I don't think you can ever achieve your full potential if you allow yourself to control others, or you allow yourself to be controlled. I want you to fulfill your divine destiny, your full potential, given to you by your Creator.

"Now the Lord is the Spirit, and where the Spirit of the Lord is, there is freedom" (2 Corinthians 3:17).

"It is for freedom that
Christ has set us free.
Stand firm, then, and do
not let yourselves be
burdened again by a
yoke of slavery"
Galatians 5:1.

Chapter 15

Money,
or How Else Can I Get Everything I Want?

When money has absolutely no meaning to you,
    you can probably have all of it you want.

When money has no power whatsoever to control you—control
your decisions, control where you go, control what you do,
control how you treat people, control who you associate with—

    Then you can probably have all of it you want.

    Then, and probably, only then.

When you're only after what the Father wants and you've set
your heart toward obedience and things eternal, then you can be
used in ways beyond your imagination.

Money controls most people. Although none of us are very
willing to admit it, it doesn't change the fact. Along with money
comes power. And that power is real. It's not at all imaginary.
With money, you can get almost anyone to do almost anything.
All it takes is money.

Money will make people do insane things, things that are illegal
and destructive to themselves and others. There are many people
who hate their lives, hate their jobs, accepting harassment, verbal
abuse, physical abuse, and yet they continue to do it day after
day, year after year, for money.

Why does money have that kind of power over us?

Because money is our god. We all learn as we grow up that to
get what we want—toys, candy, food to eat and a place to live—
we have to have money. Whoever controls the purse seems to

control just about everything. Money seems to be the answer to all things if you really look at our culture and how we idolize it.

The problem is that we've bought into the world's system as to how to live our lives, get things done and get what we want. Money defines success, period.

Money brings us honor and respect. It makes us look successful and causes us to be admired by others. We actually define who we are to other people by our financial status. We look at each other and instantly decide who the "successful" people are by what we think they have.

With money, we can do what we want, have what we want, be where we want, anytime we want it. If we want it we can just go buy it. Hire it done. Do it. We can be entertained in more ways today than anyone could possibly have imagined just a few years ago.

And if we don't have the cash for it today, no problem. We can always charge it on a credit card. That's what everybody else does, right? That makes it okay, right? Wrong. The cost of this is so much more than just dollars.

> Having money often destroys our motivation to be creative.

Money takes away our conscious need for God and our hunger for his voice. If we have money, we don't need discipline. When we have money, we don't need to be creative. We don't even need to try. Why even think about it? Just throw enough money at it and sooner or later it'll be okay.

Why do anything else? Thinking and creativity take effort, time, organizational skills, energy and discipline.

We think money will make us happy, bring us contentment and fulfillment. We think it'll satisfy the longing in our soul.

That's why we have to choose. Do we serve God or money? Jesus said so plainly in Matthew 6:24, "No one can serve two masters. Either he will hate the one and love the other, or he will be devoted to the one and despise the other. You cannot serve both God and Money." Did you notice the NIV Bible capitalizes the word "Money" in that verse?

You cannot serve both God and money. You'll live your life for money with God simply being an appendage, or you'll mature to the point that your only quest in life is to *know* God. There is no in-between.

Do we go the way of the world to get our needs met and achieve "success," or do we opt out of the world's system and partner with God, allowing him to direct us, and utilize all of our gifts, skills, abilities and talents, to meet our needs? We all do one or the other. There is no gray area or walking the fence in this. There is no compromise.

I started telling God I wanted to know what it meant to serve him and not money. The Bible clearly told me in Matthew 6 that I couldn't serve both. I challenged myself on this over and over and decided I didn't know

> I told him I was opting out of the world's system of money being first in my life, whatever that meant, wherever that took me, whatever the consequences.

what it meant to not serve money. So I decided to find out.

I bought into the belief that he is my God and if I can hear his voice, he will provide for me by telling me what to do, where to go and what to say. He knows I am not timid in trying to obey him when I believe he is directing me. He knows my level of maturity, my level of diligence and my depth of character. He knows how to connect me with others in relationship. He knows how to get me information. He knows all of my skills, abilities, gifts, talents, assets and liabilities. He knows how to connect me with wisdom, knowledge and understanding so that all of these things come together synergistically, so that I will have revenue streams to sustain my family financially, while doing what he wants me to do.

I remember the day I cut up my credit cards which I'd been virtually living on. I told God that I believed my ability to always use credit pre-empted him from moving in my life because I was always going to credit rather than to him to get my financial needs met.

Somehow, I believed. I believed and I knew I believed. And if I did whatever I was doing in the wrong way, I trusted in his ability to correct me and correct my course. I knew he would correct me because I kept on and on asking him to.

Once you mature to the point that money is no longer something you seek, but it's only a resulting by-product of the relationship you're enjoying in your adventure with the Holy Spirit, you may be able to handle some of it without it corrupting you.

> Money is simply a tool. It has no meaning to God.

As you point your destiny to partnership with him, he'll entrust you with more and more and then test your heart and your character to see if there's real growth. And if there isn't, then you're going to go around that mountain, one more time, wandering in your desert, year after year.

Money has ruined more people than we could ever count because they haven't had the character to keep it from changing them. Can you handle wealth? Be careful now. If you say an unequivocal "yes," then you can't. Guaranteed. You don't even have a clue how it will really affect you. You're unaware of the trials and temptations that will come to you because of it.

Money is simply a tool. It has no meaning to God. Money is a tangible commodity and has no life of its own.

There are those that preach that God will make you rich. They usually preach a gospel of abundance without discipline. They say give your money to God, which they usually mean give it to them, and they promise you that all sorts of wonderful things will begin to happen in your life. Many variations of this are preached throughout our world every day.

Don't be deceived by, "...Men of corrupt mind, who have been robbed of the truth and who think that godliness is a means to financial gain" (1 Timothy 6:5).

Any time we seek to exploit our relationship with God for our personal gain, seeking his presents rather than his presence, our destiny is delayed. We get a counterfeit gospel. We're deceived. Discouragement and disillusionment will eventually set in. God cannot be just a tool for us to get to the next step.

Giving is important, but give out of love, not because of rules, duty, emotional impulse or the expectations of man. Giving out of our love is giving from the heart. And this is real giving. A lover is a giver.

"For God so loved the world that he gave his one and only Son..." says John 3:16. God didn't give because of impulse, pressure, guilt, need or because someone told him he had to give. He gave *only* because he loved.

Motive is everything in the spirit. Our motives must be pure. True, God-based love is the purest motive of all.

There are some who teach that we should seek wealth to finance the gospel. I think there is a fundamental, fatal flaw in this theory. I believe the central core of this motivation is wrong. I don't think we should seek wealth. We must seek to know God; to know his voice and simply obey him. Otherwise, we have the cart before the horse. If we're seeking wealth to help God out, I think we've missed him. *It's an issue of primary focus.*

Do you think the Almighty God, Creator of heaven and earth and everything in it, needs money to get his message out? I don't. I don't think God needs money. I think we need money. Money

111

is a tool. I think he needs people that will use the tools he brings them like he wants them to be used, doing what he wants done.

Thinking that God needs money to get his message out, or that he needs us to be wealthy to finance the gospel, finance HIS gospel, his harvest, his work, is putting God into our box, subjecting him to our realm and our thinking with our limitations.

It seems to me that there's a lot more focus on the acquisition of wealth, for whatever purpose, in the church today, than there is on knowing God! I think there's something seriously wrong here. Are we focusing on God or on money?

If all the time, effort, energy and money that's being spent to preach to people about money, wealth and prosperity was spent in getting people to truly *know* God, *know* his voice, *know* his word, *know* the Holy Spirit, *in personal, direct relationship with him*, we'd see a lot more people *with* prosperity. Lots more.

We get so clever in cloaking our desire for money and justifying it in religious terms. Let's grow up. Let's get our eyes on Jesus and not money. Money does not solve problems. Money temporarily relieves the symptoms of problems.

I repeat, money does not solve problems. More often than not, it creates them, because we take the money and do what we want with it rather than waiting on God and letting him direct us what to do with it.

> Seek money and you'll never have the character of God in your heart to handle it. Period.

God does not use money to solve problems. God is not looking for money. God does not need money! God needs people he can direct, connect and impart into them his revelation and his ways of accomplishing what he wants done.

We're the ones always going to money to take advantage of situations we perceive as opportunities.

I believe God solves problems with creativity, character and relationship. All three of these flow from him to us as we seek to know him and spend time with him in the secret place. It's all about relationship. It all flows from relationship.

As we sit at Jesus' feet in surrender, humility, worship and consecration, the Holy Spirit will tell us where to go and what to do. I believe God is seeking men and women he can trust, people with pure hearts and pure motives, people who fear God and know him—people that will simply do what he tells them to do.

It's a direct relationship, not through any other man. Then it's no longer just book knowledge. Want your life to be more exciting? You'll find it in God—direct. Nothing else compares.

As our relationship with him flourishes, his manifest presence will bring about creativity in us in ways we've not imagined before. Knowledge of witty inventions will come to us. New relationships will be established. God is the master "networker." His voice will connect and correct and we will mature.

> Motive is everything is the spirit. Our motives must be pure before him.

We'll suddenly know how to do certain things. We'll have revelation wisdom come to us in dreams and visions and times in his presence that will facilitate the development of multiple revenue streams that will be a by-product of our relationship with him. Abundance is a by-product of relationship. But all our focus must be, and stay, on him, not money.

Do we need money? Yes. Do we need wisdom? Yes. But we need wisdom a whole lot more than we need money. Where wisdom is, there is no lack. Where is wisdom? "My purpose is that they may be encouraged in heart and united in love, so that they may have the full riches of complete understanding, in order that they may know the mystery of God, namely, *Christ, in whom are hidden all the treasures of wisdom and knowledge*"(Colossians 2:2-3). Give me Jesus. Wisdom, knowledge and understanding are in the personhood of Jesus the living Christ.

Do you want monetary riches or true wealth? Are they the same thing? Not at all. What is wealth? Wealth is knowing God; knowing Jesus and accepting him into our hearts, putting him on the throne of our values and decision-making; and knowing the Holy Spirit. Wealth is being in right relationship with our Creator. Wealth is knowing his voice. Wealth is knowing his presence.

Wealth is peace with God, peace with our family, divine health, loving relationships, energy and the ability to work and fulfill our God-given destiny. Wealth is sharing life with my wife that I still adore after twenty-three years of marriage.

Wealth is having my seventeen-year-old son tell me I'm his best friend and that he would rather spend a hour or two with me than any other person he knows. Wealth is laughing and enjoying times with my nineteen-year-old daughter on "date nights" together and still being confidantes.

> Give me Jesus. Let me know the Father, let me know his Holy Spirit. Let me know his presence, his smile, his voice, his ways. Nothing on this earth compares with this.

Wealth is knowing that you don't have to go through any other man to talk with God or be in his presence and get to know him. Wealth is knowing him and knowing you have clean hands and a pure heart before him. Wealth is peace. Wealth is so much more than just money.

God is more interested in transforming us to conform to the image of his Son than all the gold on the planet. Understand people matter to God. Money has no value to God whatsoever. Money is a tool.

114

I love the little story of the wealthy man who was dying and got his family to promise to put his gold in his casket so he could take it with him to heaven. They did so. When the man got to the gates of heaven, St. Peter asked him, "Well now, what are you doing up here with all that road-paving material?"

Seek to know God. Seek to fulfill your divine destiny. That may deal with great wealth, but don't make wealth your primary objective. Make Jesus your primary objective.

> A lover is a giver. Give out of love, not rules, duty or the expectations of man.

As you get closer to God, your values will increasingly be of another kingdom.

The more we turn our hearts toward truly knowing God and help others in our sphere of influence to do the same, the more we'll see the purposes of God established, "Not by might nor by power, but by my Spirit, says the Lord Almighty" (Zechariah 4:6).

I call you to no longer serve money, but to serve God.

You come to me and begin trusting me ultimately,
and I will reveal myself.

Is there anything I would rather do than reveal myself
to my people, the creation of my hands?

Come now, come apart and listen to me, to me.

To ME.

And I will gladly, lovingly share with you the secrets
in my heart.

I look about the earth all the time for people who want me,
want to know me and are willing to set aside religion,
money and prestige,

whatever makes them look good in the eyes of men,

to take time with me.

Chapter 16

Going to the Next Level

Are you really excited about your quest to partner with God and do what you're born for?

Is everything going your way and lining up for you?

Is everyone with you and encouraging you?

Feel like this is a cinch? No problems?

Well, you're probably not on the right track.

I'd like to give you a more encouraging report, but my experience tells me that there's usually a desert you'll pass through on the way to your promised land.

There's always a price to be paid to reach your potential in God. Jesus paid the price at Calvary for our sin and enabled us to be reconciled with God. We pay a price to allow God to strip out of us the ways of man, of money, of religion and tradition so that we can clearly hear his voice and partner with him to do his will.

When Jesus' earthly ministry began at age thirty, he was baptized by John the Baptist, and then what happened? The Spirit of the Lord led him into the wilderness, the desert, for forty days where he fasted and was tempted by the devil.

Moses fled Egypt and spent forty years in his desert before God spoke to him in the burning bush to go lead the Israelites to freedom.

The Israelites, led by Moses out of Egypt, on the way to their promised land, had to pass through their desert.

They wandered around and around in that desert because they didn't stay focused on God. Only a few months went by before they began grumbling and some wished they could go back to the bondage of Egypt. You see, though the bondage in Egypt was oppressive to them, there was a comfort in it because it was an environment that was known to them. They had been there four hundred years. There were no surprises there. It required no faith to remain there. It required no warfare to remain there.

But now, oh, a different story. It was necessary to believe in their destiny, to have faith and even fight for it.

Remember, the children of Israel could have gone in and possessed their promised land. They had been given the freedom to leave Egypt and they had crossed the desert. They now stood at the threshold of their promised land, but after the twelve spies went in and brought back a report of giants in the land, and ten of the spies said they were as grasshoppers in the sight of the giants, the people lost faith. This was *after* God told them that he would drive out their enemies. See Exodus 23:27-30. The children of Israel didn't believe him. That unbelief cost them.

> Every person who had been set free died in the desert, just outside their promised land, except the two that believed they could possess it.

The cost? Oh...the cost was so very high. The cost of that unbelief was that none of the people that had gained their freedom from Egypt entered into *the* promised land that was right there before their eyes, prepared *for them*, except for the two spies who believed they all could still overcome the giants and possess it. There it was.

All the people wanted to waltz into their promised land without having to fight for it. But I guess people today are the same. Who wants to fight for their promised land when they are safe in the arms of money? I'll tell you. It's the people who have opened their hearts to God, tasted of his incomparable presence and realized there's a whole lot more to knowing God than just what takes place in church.

Partnership with him is a lifestyle that permeates all that we are and all that we do.

You will have to fight to reach your divine destiny, to go to the next level in your life, to partnership with the Almighty God. I think the best example of this is our father Abraham and the way God took him to the next level.

Abraham sought to know God, learned his voice, and what did God do? He told Abraham to leave his home and go to a place "that I will show you." Can you imagine that? Check it out in Genesis 12.

Abraham had lived in the city of Ur, the most developed center of commerce in that part of the world. And yet, God called him out of that place of great plenty, straight into the desert. Worse yet, when Abraham got to the place, the entire region was in the midst of a famine!

God wanted Abraham's reliance on him, not what he had been comfortable with, not money, not the world of commerce as he had known it—God wanted Abraham's reliance on him alone. God wanted to be involved with him and lead him.

As you enter this most wonderful adventure with God, at some point he will ask you to go to a land "that he will show you." That may be simple and easy or hard and complex. But God understands process. He understands growth and the maturing process and will ask nothing of you that you cannot do.

The land "that I will show you" is where simple, childlike trust and faith comes in. Faith in his reality. Faith in his Word. Faith that you can hear him and obey. Faith in him as loving father and everlasting provider. Faith in that promise that he is a rewarder of those who diligently seek him.

119

"And without faith it is impossible to please God, because anyone who comes to him must believe that he exists and that he rewards those who earnestly seek him" (Hebrews 11:6).

> I was no longer satisfied to just sit in a pew with someone else telling me about the promised land.

I had no idea whatsoever, believe me, of the battles that I would face when I began pursuing God to let me do whatever it was that I was born for. Did he answer my prayer with giving me things on a silver platter? No, not at all. More business? No. More money? No. More notoriety or prestige? No. "Prosperity?" No. All the things I wanted? No. It seemed almost as if it were the opposite.

But all the while, our relationship became stronger. He was there waiting on me. He was there all the time. But now, I was pursuing him. He was there. My times of prayer and being in his presence became the glue that held me together and let me know he had hold of my hand as we walked down this path together. I began to learn what a drink offering was. I began to really know what it is to have the Holy Spirit as my teacher.

There were times of ecstasy, euphoria, joy unspeakable and full of glory. There were times that the heavens seemed as brass and I felt as if I was an outcast. There were times that I cried myself to sleep, with tears running down my face, filling my ears.

But all the time, somehow, I knew. I knew I believed and I was willing to risk my life, all that I was and all that I had, to persevere, to fight, to know him for who he is, not being satisfied to just know about him. I was no longer satisfied to just "make a living." I was no longer satisfied to just sit in a pew with someone else telling me about the promised land.

I decided I was going to the promised land. No matter what it looked like, no matter what it cost me, no matter who that associated me with or where it took me.

What is the promised land? It is partnership with God. It is where I *know* him—not like I knew him before. I had accepted him as my Lord and Savior. I prayed. I gave. I volunteered. I helped people. I read my Bible. I tried to do everything they told me to do. I've tried so very hard, haven't you?

But I *knew* there was more. I *knew* there was another whole realm to operate in that was right there in front of me, but I'd never possessed it.

I began to realize that the realm I'm talking about is not in some other country, it's right here in my daily life. It's a realm of what I see, feel, know and experience every day as I walk out my life in the businesses I consult with, at home with my wife and kids, and as I pray in my back yard dancing around and jumping on my trampoline.

> The secret place is where all self-consciousness is gone in your time of worship.

It's a realm of freedom in the Spirit of God that is within me. The eyes and ears of my spirit became more open and aware of his precious presence, his peace, his protection, his provision, and his promotion.

It's a realm where I began to understand that he's not there just to give me gifts and provide me comfort, but he's there with me in every aspect of my life.

It's a realm where I began to understand that without trials and temptations, there are no triumphs. There is no maturity. I began to understand what faith is and what it isn't.

It's a realm of partnership that I want you to make the quest of your life. It is your promised land.

As you start seeking God, to know God, he will make himself known to you. Not often instantly, but inevitably. All of a sudden, you'll recognize it. You'll recognize him.

The secret to this balance, the secret to knowing the next step, the secret to this quest you and I have to fulfill our destiny, is in the secret place. The secret place is where you go to "abide in him." This is where no other person exists. This is where it is just you and him and you worship, truly worship, pouring out all of who and what you are before him.

In worship and adoration of the living Christ, laying your life at the foot of the Cross, totally, really getting to *know* him, abiding in the Vine, in the secret place, is the place of power.

Your primary source of strength? The secret place.

Get in the secret place with him alone. Let him create through you. Go create value in business. Business is ministry. Business is "ministry." Business is a high calling of God. Go create value. Business is value created.

> A lot of traditional models of operation have long since passed their season and must give way to what God is doing now.

Be very careful about doing your dream in a non-profit manner, overlaying what you want to do with a bunch of religious verbiage, with your hands out to people all the time asking for their money. Unless God directs you otherwise, be for-profit. Go create value and let people pay for it. That's what business is. Business is value created. God is the Creator and he likes to create. Let God create through you. Let him create value through you. Partner with God to do business.

You can hear and live out God's guidance to you in business touching countless people and giving you a sphere of influence you never dreamed possible. Business will give you a platform to share in and share from, beyond your wildest dreams, if you'll let him.

We've been satisfied with marbles and Tinker toys when we could have been developing cities, building homes and factories, creating new inventions and doing it all in God honoring ways, as unto the Lord, and impacting our country in ways we now only dream about. All that wisdom comes from God.

Knowledge of witty inventions comes from God. How about rephrasing that this way—technology comes from God. If you have a problem with that statement, try doing a word study in your Bible searching out all the scriptures that deal with wisdom, knowledge and understanding.

As God continues to rain on the just and the unjust, with wisdom crying in the streets to be heard, please listen. Please embrace all that he gives you. Don't leave all the wisdom of future inventions and technology to the godless. Please.

I want you to go into every man's world, taking the wisdom of God, the knowledge of Christ and the understanding of the Holy Spirit with you. Wisdom, Knowledge and Understanding—take them with you into every venue of every nation. Don't limit them in your life. Give them place, space, time and honor in your life. And your reward…oh…*your rewards*…will be so great, so very great—beyond your present imagination.

You always begin with what you've got. Whatever that is. You begin. If all you can do is write out your vision, well, that's one of the very first steps anyway. Do it.

Several years ago, a friend of mine was working on a project that, in the natural seemed hopeless to him. But he felt God speak to him and say, "If you'll pick up your pencil on this project every day, I will move this project forward."

Begin taking baby steps toward your dream. I want you to "pick up your pencil" on your project *every day*, even if it's only for a few minutes, and seek his help to move it forward.

Madeline Manning Mims, the great four-time Olympic gold-medal-winning runner told us that, years ago as a teenager, she got up to run one day but she just didn't want to. She started lamenting to God that all her friends were out having fun instead of doing all this training. She said God spoke to her and said, "Yes, Madeline, but they're not going where you're going."

I want to assure you, you are not where you're going. *There's more for you, and you know it.* You know it deep down inside you. You've probably known it for years.

We've studied and taken lessons for years. Now is the time of the liberation of the common man who wants to truly partner, not with another man, but with the living God. Now is the time my friend.

All our old rules are changing. The roles are changing. How business is done, where it's done, when it's done and who does it, is changing. I don't want you left out or left behind. God's love for us and his character change not, but his ways and methods change continually. Learn from the past but embrace the future.

> Learn from the past but embrace the future.

God has so very much to share with those who will seek him, who will sit at his feet. He has entirely new models of business, of church, of effective solutions and communications.

Some time back I began to ask God what the organization chart looks like for a business that truly partners with him. About three months later, I began to get a recurring picture in my mind that I didn't even understand at first. Then all of a sudden, I understood it. He gave it to me. He's given me folders and folders full of notes about why some businesses fail and some grow. He's astounded me with what seems like volumes of information that I must get out. But, one step at a time. This is the material and the book he led me to get out first. It lays the foundation stone for the remaining works. More will come soon.

And there's more for you. There's more for you—*from his throne room to your heart*—just waiting for you to go get it. It's prepared for *you*. And, it's not too late.

God's plan for you involves an incredible amount of faith and trust. But without faith, it is impossible to please God.

You may ask, "How much faith do I need?" Well, let me answer with a story I love from Randy Hurst. In college he had a friend that was seriously intent on doing what God wanted. It was near the end of his friend's college training and a special church service was coming up that his friend began to prepare for.

When the service ended, his friend went down to the altar and knelt down. He took out pen and paper. He began to write down the following: God, I am willing to do whatever you want. I am willing to be a preacher. I am willing to be a missionary. I am willing to go to Africa for you even if they put me in a pot and boil me. I am willing to…all these things.

When he finished writing, his friend said that God spoke to him so clearly and tenderly these words. "Now turn the paper over and at the bottom of the sheet, sign your name. And I'll fill it in."

I want you to really know God. Become his friend. And do whatever he tells you to do.

"So you see, it isn't enough just to have faith. You must also do good to prove that you have it. *Faith that doesn't show itself by good works is no faith at all--it is dead and useless.* But someone may well argue, 'You say the way to God is by faith alone, plus nothing; well, I say that good works are important too, for *without good works you can't prove whether you have faith or not*; but anyone can see that I have faith by the way I act.' Are there still some among you who hold that 'only believing' is

> "Faith that doesn't show itself by good works is no faith at all--it is dead and useless."

125

enough? Believing in one God? Well, remember that the demons believe this too--so strongly that they tremble in terror! Fool!"

"When will you ever learn that 'believing' is useless without doing what God wants you to? Faith that does not result in good deeds is not real faith. Don't you remember that even our father Abraham was declared good because of what he did when he was willing to obey God, even if it meant offering his son Isaac to die on the altar? You see, *he was trusting God so much that he was willing to do whatever God told him to; his faith was made complete by what he did--by his actions*, his good deeds."

And so it happened just as the Scriptures say, that Abraham trusted God, and *the Lord declared him good in God's sight, and he was even called 'the friend of God.' So you see, a man is saved by what he does, as well as by what he believes"* (James 2:17-24 TLB. Italics by author.)

The bottom line here is James 2:24 TLB, "So you see, a man is saved by what he does, as well as by what he believes."

To say you believe, and yet not fight to possess what he has prepared for you, is deception.

You want power? You can have power.

When you can walk into meetings with kings and queens,
royalty, presidents and men and women of wealth and
power and prowess over men,

and not be swayed by their kingdom,

not be swayed, manipulated for their gain,

but be pure in heart and as wise in communication as
Nathan the prophet was with David,

You can have power.

The power that is not by might, not by this world's power,
but by the Spirit of the living, speaking God.

When you have your heart and priorities right,
Then you can walk in realms of power you never
knew existed.

He wants his place in the business world and he wants people with the character of Abraham that when he says, "Go here, go there, get up and go to a land that I will show you," they'll have the guts to go do it.

Chapter 17

The Vision of God in Business:
$$R^7 = U^X$$

My purpose, and the purpose of GodinBusiness is best stated in the two following paragraphs:

One day you will die. You will then stand alone before God. When that time comes I want you to be able to say the same thing that Jesus said to the Father in John 17:4, "I have brought you glory on earth by completing the work you gave me to do." That is what I want you to be able to say to him.

What I want you to hear from him is, "Well done, thou good and faithful servant: thou hast been faithful over a few things, I will make thee ruler over many things: enter thou into the joy of thy lord" (Matthew 25:21).

God is so very real and he is speaking to all who will listen. You can hear him. You don't have to go through any other person to know him personally. You can do what you're called to do. The ability to do it is in the call. You can do it.

You can do it whether you have any money or not. You can do it whether you have anyone to help you or agree with you or not. God is your source—not people, not money.

As you seek God you will find him. He will make himself known to you. Proverbs 8:17 says, "I love those who love me, and those who seek me find me." Jeremiah 29:12-13 says, "'You will seek me and find me when you seek me with all your heart. I will be found by you,' declares the LORD...."

In our quest to really know him and do what we're born for, we will cross many stretches of life that seem like deserts to us.

These deserts help form our Godly character and mature us and teach us dependence on him rather than reliance on ourselves.

Getting to know God is the most exciting opportunity we have in our human life.

Do not forfeit God's invitation to partner with him. Seize the opportunities that his hand has crafted for you. It is not just one big decision, it's a lifetime of discipline, discipleship, obedience and tenacity to know him through the years. It's a process. And it's worth it all.

God's will for your life will not happen automatically. You must decide you want it. Get hungry for it. Make it your quest. Ask, and keep on asking him for it. You will choose, day after day, to spend time with him, alone, in the secret place with him. It will happen *only* if you spend time with him. He must be the priority of your life.

God's plan for your life is your potential. It is not cast in stone. It's your choice. If you've never failed, you've never pushed your limits. Don't be afraid of failure. Be afraid of not obeying.

Keep that vision before you of when you will stand before God and think about what you'll say and what he'll say. When you fail, get up and keep going. Never give up. You can do this.

Keep that vision before you of when you will stand before God and think about what you'll say and what he'll say.

Pursue excellence in whatever you do, taking responsibility for your actions, being accountable, and using all the tools God has given you.

As you receive revelation and respond to it, it's natural to look at any role models that may exist. Learn from them. It's encouraging to look at others who have paid the price to receive the rewards of partnering with the living God.

130

And as your **R**elationship with God grows closer, your godly character will mature. You will be continuously receiving and **R**esponding to **R**evelation, evaluating and learning from **R**ole models, searching out and providing new **R**esources, for yourself and others, and the **R**esult will be the **R**eproduction of this journey, this process, that helped you into life's greatest adventure—this partnership with God.

You'll want to share this with others—not later, but now, as you travel every step of the way. As you're experiencing growth in this partnership with God, reproduce that same growth in others.

As you reproduce in others the same growth that you're experiencing, you'll wind up calling on all of your gifts to do this effectively. At some time or other, you'll use all of your natural gifts and your spiritual gifts to do this.

The more you use all that God has given you to do this, the more un-stopped-up you'll become. The more un-stopped-up you become the more freedom you experience.

And you won't be doing this out of duty, obligation, rules or the expectations of any other man. You'll be doing this out of love. Your motive in all of it will be love. Don't do any of this out of a sense of obligation, guilt or anything man may put on you. Operate your life out of love—loving people for who they are, not what they can do for you—sharing with them your life, just as naturally as 1,2,3, or speaking to your best friend.

Choose to do life together with people where you love them and lift them. Share life together. Share your experiences and the excitement of truly learning the application of God's Word to your daily workplace. Share who you are and what God is doing in your life. No man can take from you the freedom that God gives you as you walk out your pursuit of your divine destiny.

Don't be little and petty and protective of your little area or strut around like you're someone special. Let the life and love of Jesus Christ flow into you and through you to others. Study the scriptures, especially the books of Proverbs, Genesis, Matthew, Mark, Luke, John and Acts. Second Timothy 2:15 says, "Work hard so God can say to you, 'Well done.' Be a good workman, one who does not need to be ashamed when God examines your work. *Know what his Word says and means.*" Emphasis mine.

As you do these things, I assure you, the size of your "world" will expand. God will bring you into relationship with him as you sit as his feet and his Holy Spirit will teach you, one on one.

Then he will bring you into relationship with others so you can respond by expanding their world. He'll bring you resources to propel you in your partnership with him. Role models will come across your path you can learn from. Learn from them and mature and operate with righteousness and integrity. Allow others to see you do it, so you can be role models for others in your wake.

Jesus told us in Matthew 5:14-16, "You are the light of the world. A city on a hill cannot be hidden. Neither do people light a lamp and put it under a bowl. Instead they put it on its stand, and it gives light to everyone in the house. In the same way, *let your light shine before men, that they may see* your good deeds and praise your Father in heaven." Emphasis mine.

Results of all these things moving forward in your life will bring such joy, innovation and creativity. Life will be more exciting and fulfilling. Results will be birthed forth in the natural and in the spirit.

The power in right **R**elationships propel **R**esponses in you that bring you **R**evelation, **R**esources and **R**ole models to help produce synergistic **R**esults in your life, to birth forth **R**eproduction.

As you grow in your quest for maturity and freedom—
Doing what you were born to do—
Partnering with the living God to do it—

You'll want to reproduce your **R**elationship with God in others.
You'll want to reproduce your **R**evelation in others.
You'll want to reproduce your **R**esponses in others.
You'll want to reproduce your **R**ole models in others.
You'll want to reproduce your **R**esources with others.
You'll want to reproduce your **R**esults in others.
You'll want to reproduce your **R**eproduction in others, for we are all born to reproduce ourselves in others.

I'll abbreviate this process as $\mathbf{R}^7 = \mathbf{U}^X$.

$\mathbf{R}^7$ is the multiplication of relationships, revelation, response, role models, resources, results and reproduction…

and $\mathbf{U}^X$ is you the reader (**U**), expanded to the **X** power.

U is you—the **U**n-stopped-up you. Yes, you reading this book, expanded beyond just the natural realm.

How much can you expand to, accomplish, and achieve in your partnership with God? Exponentially.

X represents the synergy factor of you in true partnership with the Holy Spirit *bringing about exponential results.*

X is limited only by your hunger to truly know God, to help people be free, and partner with him.

Eye has not seen, nor has ear heard, nor has it entered into the heart of man what God has in store for those who will truly lay down their life, in order to get up and partner with the Holy Spirit of the living, speaking God.

Never forget $\mathbf{R}^7 = \mathbf{U}^X$.
Always remember $\mathbf{R}^7 = \mathbf{U}^X$.

We are born to reproduce. When you're reproducing in others what God has done in your life, you're fulfilled. It's automatic. Your natural and your spiritual gifts are being used like a hand in a glove. He's given you both of them. Exhilaration radiates from you. There's a flow of the Spirit of God through you that helps you grow, learn, mature, advance and have the time of your life. You begin to realize, you *are* getting to know HIM.

Now is the time. You're the generation. Make the choice. Never look back. Come unto him as a little child, humbly, trusting him with all that you are, and all that you'll ever be, all that you have, and all that you'll ever have, and accelerate your adventure with him.

I want you to experience the glory of God on your floor humbly before him. I want you to go out and do great exploits where he has you now and where he takes you.

Jesus said in Luke 18:17, "I tell you the truth, anyone who will not receive the kingdom of God like a little child will never enter it." God is waiting on you. You may think you're waiting on God but he's waiting on you.

He's with you right now, even now, saying, "Come. I will be with you and I will show you the way." On your knees, on your face, say, "Here I am. Use me Lord. I believe. Help thou my unbelief." And you know what? He will. For he is, and he is a rewarder of all who diligently seek him.

Where are you going?
$$R^7 = U^X.$$

Where are you going?
...to the land that he'll show you.

What do you think? Are you ready?
He's ready.

See-
I am doing a new thing.
Will you let me move through you? Will you?

I am singing new songs—I am creating them.
I am writing new books.
I am creating new opportunities.
I am creating.
Will you let me create through you?

The model of church is changing—
The model of who does what is changing—
The model of my leaders is changing—

And those who won't change will be left behind
in the new things that I do.

They have a choice.

It is few that go on with me and pursue continuing,
deepening, relationship with me and hear my voice.

I am creative.
I love to create.

Will you let me create through you?

The wealth of the wicked will not be transferred to the
righteous by means that we're accustomed to.

Behold, I am God and my nature is to create.

I am tired of my people being so boring and being satisfied with so little.

I have so much to give.

I am God.
  Did I not frame the worlds?
  Did I not make man?
  Did I not make man for ME?

Why would I withhold from him my ability to let him know me and let my power flow through him to do the things I like to do?

I like to create—
  I'm tired of not creating.
    I like to create.

Will you let me create through you? Create value?
Create things—ways you've not dreamed of.

Will you? Will you? Will you?
I am waiting—waiting.

The choice is yours.

Have I not given all of my gifts to man?
Have I—oh so blind?

You can have what you want—
    Haven't I said that over and over?

I gave gifts to man—
    They have chosen to operate without them.

But I have my remnant—

And my remnant will increase
    for I am doing new things, says God.

And I call out to you to let me do them through you.
    The choice is yours.

Will you humble yourself so you can be exalted?

Will you? Will you? I am waiting.

See I have anointed you to write this and you know it.
You feel my presence. These things are above you.

Will I not bring my anointing to those who seek me?

Nothing pleases me more than to share my presence.

Will you let me share my presence with you?

Will you? Will you? I am waiting.

You have a choice.

No one desires
relationship with another
person as much as our
Creator desires
relationship with us—
his creation.

Chapter 18

The Invitation–
Go Create Value

The invitation is before you now to join the GodinBusiness revolution and go create value by doing what's in your heart, afresh and anew, partnering with God to do it.

I want you to get over the fixed income mentality. Get over the fact that you may have little or no money and no one to help you. Get over the circumstances that you find yourself in and begin looking through the eyes of God and his potential for your life. Get a long-term perspective of your life and where you're going.

This is a new day, a new season, a new dispensation. Never before in the history of man has the common man had so much potential.

When Jesus told the disciples to cast their net on the other side of the boat after they had spent hours fishing and caught nothing, they simply obeyed and wham! What a catch! They caught so many fish that they could not get them all in the boat and wound up towing the net full of fish to shore. (John 21:6-8).

Now what was different about what they did before Jesus spoke and afterwards? They were using the same boat, the same net, in the same place, with the same

> Remember, even a one degree change in the course of a ship, though imperceptible for awhile, will result in that ship arriving at a totally different destination.

people. They were using the same tools in the same industry, operating the way they always had. But! They had a word of direction from the Master and the *results* were suddenly very, very different. The *yield* was more than they'd ever had before.

That's what you call synergy. And that same synergy is available to you and to me, just ordinary, common people who decide we want to do what it takes to partner with God.

The time is now. We're the generation. You're the generation. Irrespective of race, gender, or church preference, God is moving into the business arena like never before. Whether you're Protestant, Jewish, Catholic, or ...this is one incredibly exciting time to be alive and be an integral part of what God is doing today.

I am totally confident that many of you reading this are destined to achieve things beyond your wildest expectations as you truly seek to partner with God.

1 Corinthians 2:9 says, "...No eye has seen, no ear has heard, no mind has conceived what God has prepared for those who love him...." And no, I don't believe that verse only applies to the hereafter. I believe it applies today to anyone who partners with God to hear his voice and obey him.

Remember the name Gutenberg? Johannes Gutenberg, who constructed the first printing press—an invention that changed the world—wrote over five hundred years ago: "God suffers because there are multitudes whom His Word cannot reach. Religious truth is held captive in a small number of manuscripts which guard the treasures. *Let us break the seals and give wings to the truth, that it may fly to every soul born in the world.*" Where did he get the wisdom to build that first printing press? God.

> God will be transforming you into his image, re-establishing priorities, and forging your character.
> He will begin showing you opportunities to help people and often, to make money. And they'll almost always be a bit different than what you anticipated.

I want to expand your thinking. You have so very much more creativity inside you than you've ever drawn on.

Most business people rely on their own abilities to achieve what they achieve. They rely upon themselves, as opposed to relying on God. But God has a more excellent way for those who will surrender the throne of their business decision-making to him, acknowledging him in all they put their hand to. God has so much more to share with his creation.

The closer you get to God the more your spiritual gifts will come out and the more effective and enhanced your natural gifts, skills and talents will become.

The best letter has not been written yet. The best computer hasn't been built yet. The best song has not been written yet. The best sermon has not yet been preached. The best car has not been built yet. The best clerk has not clerked yet. The best CEO has not CEO'd like he can do in the future. The greatest inventions have not been invented yet. The best company has not yet been founded.

> The best way to build a team and empower them, utilizing all their skills, gifts, abilities and talents hasn't even been touched yet.

I find it so interesting that, over all the years I've pursued this passion of God in business, the only person I felt God has ever told me to learn about was George Washington Carver. I have several books about him we purchased when we went to his memorial in Missouri. He was a humble man who came up with over three hundred valuable uses for the peanut. His inventions and discoveries spawned industries, fed thousands, and changed many, many lives. Every morning he would walk and talk with God. He said it all came from his times with God.

As we spend time with him and get to know God, he will be continually transforming us into his image, re-establishing priorities and forging our character. And then when we're ready, he'll begin showing us opportunities to make money. When we won't be corrupted by what he gives us, and we can hear his voice, walk in faith, things will happen on another scale than what we've been accustomed to.

Networking has been a big buzzword in business for years now. But wait until you partner with him and allow him to network your life. You'll see it's all on a different plane with him. He's not subject to time and space, a clock or calendar. He's omnipotent and omniscient.

He'll begin taking out some of your relationships that are only baggage in your life and giving you other ones; some of which you'll touch and lift and others that will lift you and connect you in ways you could have never done alone.

On April 26, 1999, God spoke these words to me, "You don't have as much time as you had in the past. More will be compressed and accomplished in less time than in the past. I am continuing to accelerate my plan and what I'm doing. If you want to go with Me and be a part of what I am doing, you cannot be afraid. You must set your common fears aside and pursue Me and what I have for you. There is a divine synergy, a way to do more, to see more clearly, and I will give it to the hungry, those hungry to know Me, and not just have wealth for themselves."

Remember, you can hear and live out God's guidance to you in business touching countless people and giving you a sphere of influence you never dreamed possible. Business will give you a platform to share in and share from, beyond your wildest dreams, if you'll let him.

"Let your light so shine before men, *that they may see* your good works, and glorify your Father which is in heaven" (Matthew 5:16 KJV). Emphasis mine.

I want you—the ones that put God first in their lives and making a living—to be the best in the world. I want you to be sharp, innovative, creative and non-traditional. I want you to break new ground in how business is done, how it works and how it treats people. I want your own uniqueness to arise. I want the love of the Father God to flow through you to the world.

I want you to merge God…and business.

Then, when the rain comes, the streams rise, and the winds blow and beat against your life, your business, and the economy, your divine destiny will not be dependent on man, or man's economy, and you will not fall with a great crash.

"But everyone who hears these words of mine and does not put them into practice is like a foolish man who built his house on sand. The rain came down, the streams rose, and the winds blew and beat against that house, and it fell with a great crash" (Matthew 7:26-27).

Most of all, I beg you, don't do nothing. Please. The smallest acts are more important than the most admirable intentions. Act. Go get on your knees before God and give him your all.

Now unto him that is able to keep you from falling, and to present you faultless before the presence of his glory with exceeding joy....

Eye has not seen nor has it entered into your heart what he has prepared for you....

You are the generation. Birth forth in your birthright.

$R^7 = U^X$.

Go create value.

Go reproduce what God does with you in others.

I believe in you.

With sincere love,

Ted Cottingham

143

A Note From Ted

I am so happy to bring you this book. When I first began to organize notes into chapters, I thought I'd include much more about specific business operations but the more it took shape, the more I began to realize that I wasn't to help people build a second floor on a vacant lot. I had to deal with first things first.

Although I believe there is much in these pages that you can glean to help you partner with God if you want to, I'm under no illusion that you will agree with every single thing I say in here. But that's okay. I don't have all the answers.

If you can glean from these writings and benefit from my pain, confusion, surprises, unmet expectations, and all sorts of challenges in my quest to partner with God, then maybe you can start or accelerate your own partnership with him.

Whatever wisdom, knowledge, and understanding I have, I want to impart to my children, my friends, and anyone eager to learn.

I am not a master orator or master writer. I do believe God has given me much and that he's told me to write it down.

> You don't have to see everything my way. It's okay to disagree with me; we can still be friends.

Sometimes, though, I still find it difficult to articulate and give words to that which is deep within.

I have now poured out part of my heart to you, making myself vulnerable for both praise and reproof. If I have said anything in this book that hurts or offends you, I apologize. I seek to love God, love people, lift them, and see them mature with God and man. If you want to correct me on any point, you can write me at my address and I will seriously evaluate any reproof you may send.

Any of your own personal experiences about the subjects covered in this book that you'd like to share with me, I'd like to receive.

I ask that you open your heart. Be a gleaner. Glean the spirit of what I'm trying to convey. Enjoy the things I share. Search the Scriptures yourself. But most of all, seek to *know* God in a very personal relationship and do what you're born to do.

—Ted Cottingham

If you'd like a resource to help you
identify the principles brought out in this book and
put them to use in your own life…

God in Business—
A Common Man's Guide $R^7=U^X$
"Guidebook"

Fill out the following and mail or fax to GodinBusiness.com to
be notified when the $R^7=U^X$ Guidebook is available:

Name: _____

Address: _____

City: _____State: _____ Zip:_____

Phone: _____ Fax: _____

E-mail: _____

Please send more free information on:

____This book on tape and CD when available
____Consulting services
____GodinBusiness seminars

Comments on what this book meant to you: _____
_____
_____
_____
_____
_____

Thank you.
Mail or Fax to: (Fax 1-800-896-8805)
Ted Cottingham
GodinBusiness.com, Inc.
Box 33130, Tulsa, Oklahoma 74153

GodinBusiness.com, Inc.

Our purpose is to help merge
God and business and build a platform
for those who do.

Recommended Resources

Lord of the Marketplace, by Myron Rush. Victor Books. The finest book I know on the subject. Absolutely stellar resource.

Management: A Biblical Approach, by Myron Rush. Victor Books.

Praying the Scriptures, by Judson Cornwall. Creation House.

The Power of Vision, by George Barna. Regal Books.

How to Find Your Purpose in Life, Bill Greenman. Whittaker House.

The Happiest People on Earth, by Demos Shakarian. Steward Press.

God Owns My Business, by Stanley Tam. Horizon House Publishers. Excellent.

Almighty & Sons: Doing Business God's Way, by Dennis Peacocke. Box 2709, Santa Rosa, Ca. 95405. Excellent.

Business by The Book, Larry Burkett, Larry Burkett Ministries, Christian Financial Concepts. Excellent.

Discover Your Destiny, by Bill & Kathy Peel. Navpress. Superb.

Staying Close, by Dennis Rainey. Word. In a class by itself. Deals with marriage and family relationships. Of immense value to me.

Never Too Late for a New Beginning by Michael Cardone, Sr. Fleming H. Revell. I couldn't lay it down. Wonderful.

Just Business, Christian Ethics for the Marketplace by Alexander Hill. InterVarsity Press, Downers Grove, Illinois. Many wonderful examples. An incredible resource.

Your Work Matters To God, by Doug Sherman and William Hendricks. Navpress.

The Complete Christian Businessman, by Robert J. Tamasy, General Editor. Wolgemuth & Hyatt Publishers, Brentwood, Tennessee.

"Then Nathan said to David, "You are the man! This is what the LORD, the God of Israel, says: 'I anointed you king over Israel, and I delivered you from the hand of Saul. I gave your master's house to you, and your master's wives into your arms. I gave you the house of Israel and Judah.

And if all this had been too little, I would have given you even more"'" II Samuel 12:7-8.

Notes

Notes

Notes

Notes

Notes

Notes

Notes

Notes

Notes